Poetry of Relevance 2

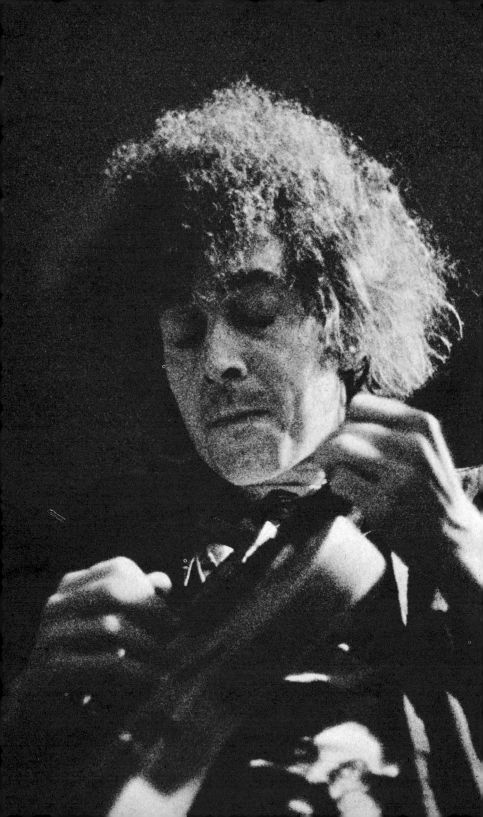

Poetry of Relevance 2

Homer Hogan
Associate Professor of English
University of Guelph

Special Consultant
Kenneth J. Weber
Assistant Professor of English
Ontario College of Education

Methuen

Toronto London
Sydney Wellington

Frontispiece: Elvin Bishop

Library of Congress Catalog Card Number 77-113485

SBN 0-458-90410-4

Designed by Carl Brett
Printed and bound in Canada
74   73   72   71   3   4   5

To the Instructor

Poetry of Relevance invites students to find significant connections between poems of our literary heritage and songs that express contemporary interests and concerns. The table of contents makes clear the general strategy: each song lyric is followed by one or more poems that develop the theme or poetic technique found in the lyric.

To take full advantage of this text, the instructor should be sure to play the recommended recording of the song preceding the poems he wishes to discuss. Once a mood is established by the recording, the ways of working from song to poem are limited only by the instructor's ingenuity. The special interest sparked by hearing the songs of such artists as John Lennon, Leonard Cohen, Paul Simon, and Joni Mitchell extends to the poetry itself.

However he proceeds, the instructor should be able to use one or more of the following features of this book: (1) the index of themes, (2) the critical approach developed in the introductions and transitional material, (3) the indexes of poets and song-writers in each volume, and (4) the *Suggestions for Study* prepared for high school students by Kenneth Weber, Assistant Professor of English at the Ontario College of Education. (The *About the Poets* section was also contributed by Professor Weber.)

Complete record information is given with each song and in the discographies at the end of books 1 and 2. Most likely, the instructor will find that about six albums will be all he needs for the semester's work in poetry. Students might be asked to buy or borrow some records of songs not used in class so that they can do independent study.

In comparing books 1 and 2, it will be noticed that although they may be used independently of one another, there are certain advantages in using both. Together they offer a much wider range of songs and poetry. Furthermore, the first volume offers a substantial amount of commentary in the introduction and transitions between sections, whereas the second keeps commentary to a minimum in order to provide a greater number of songs and poems to which the student can apply his own thinking. The introductions to the two books also complement each other. In the first book the introduction is an essay on wonder addressed mainly to the student's affective experience of literature. In the second, the introduction is more intellectually oriented, sketching out certain logical principles that students might use to help settle arguments about literary interpretations. Special topics considered in the first book include the forms of poetic development (1 *Folk Songs and Blues);* the perspectives and philosophy of New Generation songwriters (3 *Tim Buckley);* contexts of imagery (4 *Joni Mitchell);* uses of ambiguity (5 *John Lennon and the Beatles);* surrealism (11 *Robin Williamson);* and the function of myth (12 *Myth and The Ballad of Frankie Lee and Judas Priest).* A model of detailed poetic analysis is offered in the discussion of Joni Mitchell's song-poems. The relation of truth to art is touched upon in connection with an analysis of the blues in the second book (2 *John KaSandra*).

In order to make *Poetry of Relevance* useful to young people who wish to write their own songs and poems, I place particular emphasis on the ways that poetry and song *move* an audience and keep technical terminology at an absolute minimum. I also include song lyrics and poems that vary considerably in quality and effectiveness so that instructors can challenge students to discover why one song or poem works better than another, thereby unearthing secrets of the writer's craft.

Contemporary Canadian, British, and American poetry accounts for about half of the poems in the books; the remainder represent the major periods of British and North American poetic literature. Some of the contemporary poems are by high school and college students. Of special importance is the attention paid to the poetry of the black people of North America. The books include not only some powerful examples of traditional blues lyrics and songs by Jerry Moore, Bukka White, John Kasandra, and the Rev. F. D. Kirkpatrick, but also poems by Langston Hughes, Gwendolyn Brooks, Bob Kaufman, Margaret Walker, Dudley Randall, Robert J. Abrams, Donald Jeffrey Hayes, Calvin C. Hernton, M. Carl Holman, Lucy Smith, Paul Vesey, and Dr. Martin Luther King, whose oratory, as I hope to show, often rises to the level of poetry.

Acknowledgments

With great pleasure, I offer my profound thanks to Joni Mitchell, who first encouraged me to begin this project; my wife Dorothy, whose musical knowledge was an invaluable resource; Mr. Jay Mark of TRO; and most of all, my friend and colleague, Dr. Eugene Benson, whose imagination and erudition are responsible for some of the happiest combinations of songs and poems in these books, especially in the sections on John Lennon and Leonard Cohen.

H.H.
University of Guelph
March, 1970

Contents

The Logic of
Literary Explanation

How can we ever "prove" anything about literature? Isn't
it all a matter of individual preference? The student who
asks these questions deserves a fair answer. It is
impossible, within a single chapter, to do justice to the
most complicated issue they raise: the tricky problem of
making literary *evaluations,* of determining to what extent
a work is "good" or "bad". Here I shall limit myself to a
simpler but more important issue contained in the student's
sceptical questions. This is the problem of making
reasonable *explanations* or *interpretations* of literature —
the problem of showing how we can settle arguments
about what a literary work is intended to *do* or *mean,*
without recourse either to the whims of individual readers
or to such fearsome authorities as learned critics, tradition,
public opinion — and one's instructor.

The method we seek might be best introduced by
something that at first seems far removed from literary
concerns, namely, the process of reaching a *fair verdict.*
Consider what happens in a court of law when a man is
being tried for murder. The jury must decide which is true,
the defence statement that the man is innocent, or the
prosecution statement that he is guilty. How can the jurors
proceed? Clearly, they can't use the tests of mathematics
or formal logic, except in an auxiliary way. But neither can
they use experiment: obviously they cannot recreate the
situation before the murdered man died and then see
whether or not the accused kills him. Statements about
unrepeatable past events are not capable of scientific
verification, and these include not only such important
matters as questions of guilt and innocence, but also all
questions about who said what, when, and why — that is to
say, most of the concerns of practical life as well as those
of literary explanation and interpretation.

The difficulties of this situation, however, can, for practical purposes, be partially overcome. Unable to experiment, the jurors choose between the prosecutor's and the defence attorney's statements by asking themselves which lawyer has made the more convincing case. This they determine, consciously or unconsciously, by applying three criteria: (1) *accountability,* (2) *frequency,* and (3) *simplicity.* (See Monroe C. Beardsley, *Thinking Straight,* 2nd ed., Prentice-Hall, pp. 70-76.) We use the term "accountability" to refer merely to the degree that reasons — good, bad or indifferent — are offered for the existence of the data to be explained. Such a loose usage reflects the fact that a jury will reject a lawyer's case if he fails to offer any explanations as to why certain key events occurred. The second test, "frequency," refers to the degree that the reasons offered by either lawyer seem to have successfully explained similar events in the past. It marks, that is, the *probability* of the lawyer's explanations and is reinforced, for example, by the testimony of expert witnesses in the fields of ballistics and psychiatry, and in general, by the findings of experimental science. The third test, "simplicity", refers to the number of assumptions introducd by the rival attorneys in order to make their cases believable. The more that a jury is asked to *assume* to be true, the less likely it is to be persuaded.

But though the three tests of accountability, frequency, and simplicity make it possible for a jury to make decisions, we should not be too confident about this kind of reasoning. These tests are merely the dictates of common sense and are not easy to justify philosophically. Nor can the tests be weighted; we could not, for example, say that "accountability" is worth 25 per cent less than "frequency". Furthermore, because of their vagueness, these tests cannot produce consistently accurate, unambiguous results. Another reason for the questionable status of verdicts is that their soundness depends not only on the available evidence, but also on the particular people who pass the verdicts. That is to say, in the natural and physical sciences, an experiment is acceptable only if everyone who performs it can obtain the same result, whereas in law, a verdict is acceptable even though we know that not everyone would come to the same conclusion after considering the case offered by the rival lawyers. Society can only require that individual judges and jurors make a sincere, unprejudiced effort to discover the truth according to the rules of the juridical game.

What we have been saying about verdicts applies in general to all statements about unrepeatable past events, including the creation of literary works. When we want to know what a poem or song was intended to do or mean, we are in the same position as that of a judge who has to determine past actions and motives, and like him, we proceed by considering first one hypothesis, then another, asking ourselves which has the greater degree of account-ability, frequency, and simplicity. But unlike the judge, we must also be the opponents who advance the various hypotheses as well as the investigators who assemble the data, for in making our way through both life and art we are in a sense entire courts, the best of which avoid prejudice, concede fallibility, remain open to appeal, and carefully observe the rules of evidence.

In making literary judgments, however, we need two special rules in addition to the three principles described above. The first is required by the practical necessities of education. If we wish to learn from someone, what should we do when we don't understand him — blame him for talking nonsense or ourselves for being ignorant? Operating on the first assumption, we would never learn anything that wasn't immediately obvious — not even the meaning of a new word. Operating on the second, we would ask questions, think out problems, try new perspectives, and, in short, open ourselves to education. These con-siderations lead to the following principle: *always assume that discourse is meaningful and valuable until your best efforts have failed to reveal it as such.* Applied to literary study, this fundamental axiom of education means that we should *do justice* to the work before us by looking for interpretations and explanations of it that will make it seem as *good* a work as we can convincingly show it to be.

It is important to note here that this principle of doing justice to discourse is required only by the purposes of education. A reverse assumption would have to be made when our purpose is not to study, but to evaluate discourse. A critic or teacher does not give writers or students the benefit of the doubt; on the contrary, he assumes that what is not clear or appealing to him is in fact faulty, and then his job is to demonstrate this faultiness. A somewhat similar situation exists in law. In order to reach a fair verdict, judges and jurors in English-speaking countries assume a man to be innocent until proven guilty. One reason for this is that if they first assume the accused to be guilty, then in many cases the evidence for his apparent innocence could be interpreted as further evidence of his guilt: in Alice's wonderland, the knave of hearts was convicted because he looked innocent — which of course is just the way a guilty man would try to appear. On the other hand, a good investigator of crime begins by suspecting everyone capable of committing it. The moral is that practical principles of inquiry must be changed when the purposes that justify them change.

The second special principle we need in order to test literary explanations is really an application of the basic "simplicity" axiom: *always assume that what a man says or does is what he intends to say or do unless there are signs that compel you to interpret him otherwise, in which event your interpretation should introduce no more than what is necessary to be consistent with those signs.* Without using this principle, men would be unable to to communicate — every man would be free to take the words of every other man as a bit of irony or symbolism or humor regardless of what the words seemed to say, and therefore no man could expect to be understood. Fortunately, we all do more or less employ the principle in our everyday relations with one another and so achieve a rough degree of mutual understanding. In reading literature, however, many people forget this rule. Having heard that literature is "symbolic," they immediately look for something other than what is actually said in every poem or novel they read, and because a literary work can be interpreted as a reflection of almost anything else, these symbol hunters soon become unable to discuss literature rationally with other readers or even to find good reasons for changing their own minds about their literary interpretations. Once I gave my students a "poem" to contemplate that was really a laundry list. The assignment was unfair, but it produced some interesting results. One student took the list to be an indictment of man's pre-occupation with trifles; another saw in it a prophecy of what would be left of civilization after a nuclear war; and a particularly ingenious girl reconstructed from it the record of a complex domestic tragedy! But, of course, they had only touched upon the possibilities.

It should not be thought, however, that this "communication" principle is merely a limitation on non-literal readings. Actually it shows us exactly how to uncover symbolism, irony, and other meanings that lie beneath the surfaces of words. A good writer knows that he cannot reasonably hope to convey non-literal meaning to others unless he (1) provides signs that prevent readers from taking him literally, as they normally expect to do, and (2) makes the signs such that readers discover what he really intended when they account for them adequately. The communication principle directs us to these signs and hence to the keys for hidden meanings. To cite a simple example, suppose one were to hear a rock-style ballad with the title line, "Mother Always Knows Best". We could not believe the singer meant that line literally because we know the rock beat is a sign that he belongs to a generation which, happily or unhappily, has grave doubts about mother. That very fact, however, suggests his true meaning: he is being ironical, teasing us with a "put on". But there may be other facts in the verses that could only be explained by assuming that he is being ironical about this irony. This would follow, for instance, if the verses described drug experiences, in which event "mother" would be the slang for dope peddler. And in case these experiences were described negatively, we would have to reverse the title line once again, treating it this time as a kind of triple irony. Note that we would miss these interesting twists if our explanations went beyond what was necessary to account for the facts of the song, *e.g.,* if we took "mother" as referring to Mother Earth or the Virgin Mary.

Another more subtle example is a real problem in Robert Frost's poem, *Stopping by Woods on a Snowy Evening;* namely, what does Frost mean by "sleep" in the closing line, "and miles to go before I sleep"? Several facts about the context of that word are not easily explained if we limit "sleep" to its ordinary meaning. First, the word receives special emphasis because it is the repeated end of the poem. Secondly, a poem that climaxes in a state of mere drowsiness does not seem to be much of a poem, and according to our justice or education principle, we should first work on the assumption that Frost's poem has merit. In order to deal with these facts, many readers have interpreted "sleep" as having overtones suggesting death. This reading explains the special emphasis on that word, provides an interesting theme, and also squares nicely with the poem as a whole. Furthermore, it introduces only what is necessary; to interpret "sleep" as a *symbol* standing for death would carry us farther from the literal level than we need to go, for we can solve our problem simply by letting "sleep" *suggest* death.

The three criteria of accountability, frequency, and simplicity, and the special axioms to enable education and communication constitute the "logic" of literary explanation. Using them, we can choose among our guesses and make persuasive arguments in favor of our choice. But we must not forget that the final result is still only a guess, intrinsically much less supportable than the hypotheses of experimental science. Furthermore, we must be prepared to expect that several equally defensible explanations may be found for a given work — or, in fact, for any given case of human behavior.

We should also point out that the two special axioms for literary interpretation are even more untidy than the three general criteria that have previously been criticized. Take the education or "justice" axiom. When do we stop "doing our best" to understand someone and begin to evaluate him? And what should we do when there is a conflict between the education and communication principles? On the one hand, we want explanations that make a work "look good," and often this means we have to interpret it symbolically (as my students tried to do in the case of the laundry list); on the other hand, we need to keep as close as context permits to a literal reading of the text if we are to be able to choose among interpretations. Obviously, it will not be easy to reconcile these require-ments in every case. Another problem is the question of which should be decisive — what words *say,* or what the author really *intended* them to mean? Critics and aestheticians are still hotly debating this matter. (See Homer Hogan, "Hermeneutics and Folk Songs," *Journal of Aesthetics and Art Criticism,* Winter, 1969.)

The principles we have sketched above, however, can provide about as much practical guidance in literary studies as we can expect in life. In fact, they are directly relevant to life, for they apply to every situation in which we try to understand one another.

But let us now apply these principles to a typical case. Consider the following poem by William Carlos Williams:

> *The Red Wheelbarrow*
>
> So much depends
> upon
>
> a red wheel
> barrow
>
> glazed with rain
> water
>
> beside the white
> chickens

During the days of Senator Joseph McCarthy and the Red witch hunts of the fifties, many students of mine in America would nod in approval when I read them an interpretation of these lines that was written for me by a very patriotic young man. His thesis was that the "red wheelbarrow" was a symbol for communist subversion and that, consequently, "so much" referred to western civilization and "white chickens" to unsuspecting innocents like the readers of the poem. Whatever one might think of his hypothesis, his supporting arguments were certainly not without merit. Appealing to the principles of education and communication, he pointed out that the poem makes no sense unless we go beyond the given words to find out exactly what it is that "so much" refers to. But we don't have to go far, he said, to find the answer. We need only consider carefully the things that "so much" is said to depend upon. He argued that in themselves, these things — a red wheelbarrow, rain, and a few white chickens — could not possibly serve very important functions, and so they must be symbols for that which does have importance. Working then from the characteristics of the symbol to those of the symbolized, we ask what kind of an object is a wheelbarrow in a peaceful farm scene? It's an object hardly

likely to be noticed, something quite harmless, and yet,
because we are told it is of great consequence, these
appearances must be deceptive, disguises to fool those
who would be frightened if they saw it for what it truly is.
My student then declared that nothing fits this description
better than the great communist conspiracy. He added that
if there is any doubt about this identification, consider the
fact that this dangerously deceptive wheelbarrow is called
not green nor blue, but "red".

Attempting to refute this interpretation, another student
objected to the assumption that a wheelbarrow serves no
important functions. City dwellers, he said, may not
appreciate wheelbarrows, but as a farmer's son, he knows
that without such simple, unglamorous tools his father
would go out of business. The "so much" that depends
upon a wheelbarrow, then, is nothing less than the farmer's
way of life.

The second student's interpretation has the advantage of
being clearly simpler than the first; he makes sense out of
"so much" and "wheelbarrow" without introducing
symbolic meanings. A third student, however, insisted that
we could approach Williams' poem even more simply.
Why, she asked, must we make the importance of a thing a
matter of functions? Couldn't the wheelbarrow be important
simply because it's beautiful? Following this possibility,
she then showed how the wheelbarrow as it is described is
the centre of a lovely, sensuous picture of contrasting
colors, textures, and shapes. Under this perspective, one
meaning of "so much" would therefore be "so much
beauty". But the student also recognized a problem.
If Williams' poem is really such a simple thing, why
wouldn't everyone see it this way? Her answer was that
people are so involved in using things that they fail to
preceive the beauty ordinary objects may possess.
Williams, she continued, must have been trying to tease his
readers out of this blinding pre-occupation with utility when
he left the expression "so much" stand incomplete. Asking
themselves, So much what? honest and persistent readers
of his poem should find that their utilitarian notions of
importance cannot be reconciled with the image before
them; and eventually, they should also discover how
"so much" of their capacity to enjoy life depends upon

their willingness to suspend those notions so that they can perceive beauty tucked away in the corners of everyday living.

These observations carry the third student beyond her first almost literal interpretation of "so much," but they seem to introduce only what is necessary to explain two facts that prevent us from being content with it: the incomplete form of Williams' poetic statement and the difficulty that the average reader experiences in dealing with the poem. In any event, her total view of Williams' work is surely more satisfactory than that presented by the first two students. In the first place, it is the closest to the text and so is most faithful to the communication principle. But in keeping this close to the text, it also makes the poem seem much better, and hence it is the one most faithful to the "justice" or education principle. If Williams wanted to warn us against communism or to make us appreciate farming, he could certainly have chosen more efficient means for these ends; on the other hand, it is hard to imagine a more ingenious way of embarrassing us out of our blindness to the beauty of ordinary objects.

But in doing full justice to Williams' poem, the third interpretation also manages to be most successful in passing the general tests of accountability, frequency, and simplicity because it enables us (1) to distinguish the rhythms, sounds, images, stanza form, and syntax in all their rich details and cross-relations; (2) to find artistically convincing reasons for why Williams chose to use one detail of expression rather than another; and (3) to make all these distinctions and arguments demonstrate the excellence of the poem as a tightly unified diversity. How, for example, could the other hypotheses provide reasons for the fact that "barrow", "water", and "chickens" are set off in short parallel lines? Or how could they account for the brevity and sparse simplicity of the poem as a whole? These features are easily explained, however, if, in keeping with the third interpretation, we say that they bring out the simple beauty of a common scene we would normally never really see.

By sticking as close as she could to the printed page, the third student, then, was in addition not only doing justice to the poem but also developing an interpretation with a greater degree of accountability, frequency, and simplicity. This suggests that our logic of literary explanation can also provide the following guide for inquiry: *always begin by making your interpretation conform to the communication principle, for if you succeed, you will probably also make your interpretation conform to the other principles.* Such a procedure will be especially effective in dealing with literature that is good. A work is not likely to please many or to please long unless its creator has made sure that reasonable and sensitive readers can't miss the treasures he offers, and what could be better for this purpose than the directions that the text itself not only indicates but demands?

Once again, however, we must keep in mind the tentative character of literary hypotheses. The third interpretation presented above might not hold so well once we consider a fourth possibility: that Williams' poem demonstrates not how ordinary objects can be beautiful in themselves, but rather how they become beautiful when transformed by poetic techniques. But hypotheses about discourse that is art have a further restriction. As we pointed out in the Introduction in *Poetry of Relevance I,* "engagement" is an essential dimension of the experience of wonder. Artists and writers who want to release this experience in us must therefore involve us to some degree in the creation of their works. Consequently, to be effective they must always leave some latitude for interpretation and explanation, or at least some opportunity for discovery. A poem dies for us when we no longer wonder about it. Good literature, in brief, is always open-ended.

1

Bukka White and Traditional Blues

In recent years, increasing attention has been paid to the past, present, and future of the blues. LeRoi Jones' *Blues People,* Paul Oliver's *The Meaning of the Blues,* Samuel Charter's *Bluesmen,* and Charles Keil's *Urban Blues* are only a few of the excellent studies now available. One of the questions that fascinates researchers is the problem of exactly where the blues came from. No one knows the whole story. We do know that the beat and scale go back to Africa, and we have also identified some early American black music that foreshadows the blues, for example, the music of fife and drum, pan pipes, field "hollers," prison work gang chants, unaccompanied song, peddlar's calls, and the guitar and banjo playing of travelling street musicians and preachers. It isn't until about 20 years after the Civil War, however, that we find evidence of developed blues songs.

One reason it is hard to uncover the early history of the blues is that "church-going" black society refused to preserve what they considered to be "devil's music". Bukka White — born Booker T. White — describes his grandmother's reaction when he tried to learn the blues in the early 1900's:

"My grandmother done raised me, and I couldn't play no blues there in the house. Of course, I could play those old hymns and that, but if I wanted to get with my guitar and the blues I had to go way down into the woods, all on my own." (Interview by Dick Flohill, *Coda,* January, 1969, p. 3.)

In this section, *Joe Turner* and *You Don't Know My Mind* are two of the oldest known examples of this "devil's music". They are followed by Bukka White's *Fixing To Die,* composed in the oldest of the three main styles of rural blues, Mississippi Delta. The others are the Southeastern and Texas traditions. As played by their leading inter-preters, Son House and Bukka White, Delta blues are characterized by heavy, rough rhythms and singing, moans, bottle-neck guitar techniques, drone bass, and spoken introductions and closings. Bukka White says that Delta blues developed in "road houses" — shacks and barns set aside by plantation owners as places "for the Negro to have fun" on Friday evenings — until midnight, when the owners closed the doors to make sure their field hands would be ready for work at dawn.

But Delta blues had more than a social function. As Bukka White's song, *Fixing To Die,* makes clear, they could also express deep personal feeling in words and rhythms of great simplicity and power. Bukka White told me that he wrote this song shortly after the death of his mother. It is generally recognized to be one of the finest blues lyrics ever written.

Technically, the blues can be discussed in terms of form, harmonic pattern, scale, and rhythm. The earliest blues basically follows a 12-bar, 3-line form in which the first line establishes a problem or situation, emphasized by repetition in the second line and resolved by the third line. Each four-bar line is further divided roughly in half, the first half being a vocal cry and the second an instrumental response. The most common harmonic progression involves the tonic, subdominant, and dominant chords of a major key. But it is the scale that gives the blues its special character. The blues scale is neither major nor minor, but — perhaps significantly — the result of tension between the pentatonic scale of Africa reflected in the melody and the diatonic scale of the West on which the harmony is based. This tension is most marked in the "blue notes," which are somewhere in the neighborhood of a flattened 3rd, 7th, and sometimes 5th of a major scale. Indefinite in pitch, these notes give color and power to the lyric, the form, and the insistent, pulsating harmonies. The total structure is a point of departure for the blues singer who raises his song differently each time he sings it — contracting, expanding, working out new vocal and instrumental variations according to his mood and immediate feelings.

Finally, a word about the heartbeat of the blues — its rhythm. The iambic meter of natural speech sets the pattern of blues rhythm. But the accented notes have the force of hammer blows, stomping feet and passionate outcries. The beat is where the blues live.

Joe Turner

Traditional Blues

This old blues song goes back to the 1890's
and refers to Joe Turney, who was the
official in charge of moving convicts from
Memphis to the prison in Nashville.

They tell me Joe Turner's come and gone.
They tell me Joe Turner's come and gone.
Oh Lordy, got my man and gone.

He come with forty links of chain.
He come with forty links of chain.
Oh Lordy, got my man and gone.

They tell me Joe Turner's come and gone.
They tell me Joe Turner's come and gone.
Oh Lordy, done left me here to sing this song.

Come like he never come before.
Come like he never come before.
Oh Lordy, got my man and gone.

You Don't Know My Mind

Traditional Blues
Sung by Josh White
Josh White, Electra 123

You don't know, you don't know, you don't know my mind.
You don't know, you don't know my mind.
When you see me laughin', laughin' just to keep from cryin'.

You can't tell, you can't tell, you can't tell how I feel.
You can't tell, you can't tell how I feel,
With these cold iron shackles — shackles diggin' in my heel.

You can't see, you can't see, you can't see me now.
You can't see me, baby, you can't see me now,
'Cause I'm long-time gone — gone and won't be back nohow.

Fixing to Die

Words and Music by Bukka White
Bukka White, Vol. 1, Takoma 1001;
Country Blues 1, Folkways RF 1
Hear also Buffy Sainte-Marie
Many a Mile, Vanguard 79171

I'm looking far in mind, I
  b'lieve I'm fixing to die
  b'lieve I'm fixing to die
I'm looking far in mind, I
  b'lieve I'm fixing to die
I know I was born to die
  but I hate to leave my children crying

Just as sure as we living today
  sure we's born to die
  sure we's born to die
Just as sure we live
  sure we's born to die
I know I was born to die
  but I hate to leave my children crying

Your mother treated me, children, like I
  was her baby child
  was her baby child
Your mother treated me like I
  was her baby child
That's why it's I tried so hard
  to come home to die

So many nights at the fireside
  how, my children, mother would cry
  how, my children, mother would cry
So many nights at the fireside
  how, my children, mother would cry
Because I told the mother, I
  had to say good-bye

Lookover yonder
> *on the burying ground*
> *on the burying ground*

Look over yonder
> *on the burying ground*

Yonder stand ten thousand
> *standing to see them let me down*

Mother, take my children back
> *before they let me down*
> *before they let me down*

Mother, take my children back
> *'fore they let me down*

And don't leave them screaming and crying
> *on the graveyard ground*

Tichborne's Elegy, Written With His Own Hand in the Tower Before His Execution

Chidiock Tichborne

My prime of youth is but a frost of cares,
My feast of joy is but a dish of pain,
My crop of corn is but a field of tares,
And all my good is but vain hope of gain;
The day is past, and yet I saw no sun,
And now I live, and now my life is done.

My tale was heard and yet it was not told,
My fruit is fallen and yet my leaves are green,
My youth is spent and yet I am not old,
I saw the world and yet I was not seen;
My thread is cut and yet it is not spun,
And now I live, and now my life is done.

I sought my death and found it in my womb,
I looked for life and saw it was a shade,
I trod the earth and knew it was my tomb,
And now I die, and now I was but made;
My glass is full, and now my glass is run,
And now I live, and now my life is done.

2

John KaSandra and Urban Blues

We believe it is fitting that Bukka White and John KaSandra open this study of popular lyrics and that the Rev. Frederick Kirkpatrick closes it, for the work of these men presents in pure form what contemporary popular song builds upon and what it ultimately must return to when it needs new strength and honesty, namely, the blues. KaSandra, White, and Kirkpatrick convey the essential elements of the blues both musically and lyrically. Musically, KaSandra expresses the heart of urban blues; White and Kirkpatrick — pure rural blues. Lyrically, they put into words what can be heard in the music of both traditions, the sorrow, humor, dignity, endurance, anger, love of life, and passion for freedom latent in its very shape and rhythm. In brief, they show us what the blues *mean.*

But how do blues lyrics *work?* How do they make that special impact on our sense of wonder which all art requires? Basically, blues lyrics create their effects by means of what they release in the singer. In many blues songs, and especially in *soul* songs, the lyrics consist of a simple catch-word or phrase to trigger the singer's emotion; and what the audience primarily reacts to is not what the singer says, but the feeling in his voice and gestures of his face and body. There are some blues songs, however, designed not only to allow the singer freedom to express his emotions, but also to affect us directly by what they say. In these cases, blues lyrics work like poems in general. One special characteristic of blues as poetry is their emphasis on ''truth'' as a source of poetic appeal. Other kinds of poems and songs may frequently draw most heavily on imagery, prosody, drama, or fantasy for poetic effect, but blues poetry generally makes these elements subordinate to an impression of truthfulness.

The lyrics of John KaSandra are excellent examples of the important role the feeling of truth can play in blues poetry. Like the mythical Trojan princess whose name he adopts, John KaSandra—born John Anderson—believes he is doomed to tell the truth no matter how bitter it may sound;

in fact, he even considers truth to be God, believing that his duty as an artist is to make his listeners sense its claim over their consciences. Hearing his songs, one perceives immediately how they reflect this intention.

KaSandra's lyrics are also good evidence of the power of truth as a source of poetic appeal. Whether truth is a legitimate measure of poetic excellence is another question. This book is concerned with how songs and poems actually work, not with how they should be judged, and though certain academic critics may be appalled at people who respond to truth in art instead of restricting themselves to the pleasure of "pure" form, none can seriously deny that people generally are moved by truth. We now consider, therefore, some of the features of truth which make it so useful to those writers who are more interested in affecting humanity than conforming to standards.

But we must first distinguish the various senses in which "truth" operates in poetry. Basically, we can make out three kinds of poetic truth, all of which can be easily recognized in KaSandra's songs: *factual accuracy, perspective accuracy,* and *emotionally significant truth.* The song *Mose* conveys "factual accuracy" by providing cutting insight into the history of the black people of America; it projects "perspective accuracy" because it appears to reflect what would actually be said and seen by a man like Mose; and it has "emotionally significant truth" because what it reveals affects our moral sympathies. Though often working together, these kinds of truth can sometimes be experienced as distinct from one another. It frequently happens, for example, that a poem may exhibit perspective but not factual accuracy. In Browning's dramatic monologues, there is even a deliberate opposition between the two so that Browning can show how certain ways of looking at life distort reality (consider, for example, *My Last Duchess).* Another important point to be made about these three kinds of truth is that what counts is their *seeming* to be truth, and as any good liar knows, what is in fact false may appear truer than what is in fact true. Furthermore, if truth—or more precisely, the appearance of truth—is a major source of the appeal in a given poem or song, the listener should be aware that it is. Hearing a good "put down" blues or gospel song, an excited audience will shout its agreement with the observations of the singer; unless a listener feels that kind of desire to say "amen" or "yea," truth is not making itself aesthetically dominant.

With these distinctions in mind, we may proceed to the ways an impression of truthfulness can reinforce the principal effect of all successful works of art—*wonder*. We pointed out five aspects of wonder in the Introduction to Book 1—perception, unity, surprise, engagement, and discovery. In a state of wonder, *perception* is intensified because objects of wonder shine for us, stepping out of their backgrounds and appearing as they are in them- selves, rather than as mere things to be used for practical ends, or bits of information obscured by prejudice and familiarity. By making us believe he is presenting life truthfully, the writer obviously heightens this process. Why, for example, does the song *Mose* have such a powerful impact? Surely one main reason is that in experiencing the song, we feel we are perceiving for the first time the common black man as he really is; and that, of course, could not happen unless we sensed the truth of what KaSandra is presenting.

Unity, the second aspect of wonder, is that which allows us to relate everything in our experience of an art work to the object of wonder focusing our perceptions. When the writer convinces us that his work is unfolding according to the rules of truth, he creates a particularly effective basis for this condition of wonder: Mose's indictment of racism has a powerful unity because of the way its truth compels us not only to endure the logic of his bitter, ironic exposures but also to relate them to the whole course of American history. By taking advantage of what KaSandra calls the "laws of cause and effect," the author of *Mose* does not need to create a dramatic situation to give direction and unity to the course of his work; rather he finds this situation in historical fact.

The counterpart of unity is *surprise,* the third ground of wonder. Unity provides a system of expectations for organ- izing our experience; surprise constitutes the violations of that system which make this experience emotionally vital. But as we pointed out in the Introduction to Book 1, surprise should not be merely shock; on reflection, we should find that the unexpected is really a logical development of what previously took place — we should have known all along the butler did it. Making the unexepected credible necessarily involves an impression of truthfulness, and the greater that impression is, the more striking is the surprise. Thus, the most disturbing feature of Mose's surprising revelations is that they *should* be surprising, that we the listeners have overlooked or forgotten the truth in them.

Engagement, the fourth aspect of wonder, refers to the way we interpret an art work in terms of our own experience. Truth that is emotionally significant, that makes claims on our moral sense can provoke intense engagement. Because of the ethical implications of what they reveal, KaSandra's songs can keep us thinking about what they say long after the music is over.

The capacity of truth for sustaining the effect of wonder is also evident when we consider *discovery,* the last and most comprehensive stage of wonder. In the experience of discovery, all the other modes of wonder find their completion, and what could be a more enduring form of discovery than revelation of significant truth? That, in fact, is a mark of greatness in literature, as nearly everyone admits, and even in the popular song lyric, the frailest of literary forms, we can see how greatness can at least be pre-figured when a writer like John KaSandra strips away the veils of ignorance.

Finally, we should point out that truth may limit as well as reinforce the creation of wonder. To appear truthful, a poet might have to forgo the charms of brilliant, elegant language, as in the case of the blues poet whose speech must be that of ordinary working people if he is to express their thoughts and feelings with authority. Furthermore, a writer who wants to "tell it like it is," may need to root himself so deeply in a particular place and time that many will be unable to respond fully to what he says. The song *Mose,* for example, would probably not work very well for those who don't know what it feels like to oppress or be oppressed.

Mose

Words and Music by John W. Anderson
KaSandra, Capitol ST 2957

Spoken:

Y'all don't see me all hog tied,
Sleeping with tears falling from my eyes.
Y'all don't see my woman in my master's loving game
And me hanging from a rope taking his blame.
I planted his field to grow row by row,
I bet you all wouldn't believe I'm wearing his second hand clothes.
See, there's a lot of things y'all don't know;
I betcha don't know my name is Mose.

Y'all don't see this brown bag in my hand
And me waiting on the corner to git some work if I can.
Y'all don't know I see it in my mind,
Y'all done built dem machines and done left me behind.
I can see you tried to make me a two legged mule
To help the four legged ones do what you wanted them to.
I been working and serving you while you went to school to know
And y'all still don't know my name is Mose.

Y'all know what I say to my woman at night,
'Cause she checks wit you to see if I told her right.
You ask her 'bout da table and she'll tell you 'bout da door.
You trick her wit words and make her tell you what you wanna know,
What y'all done y'all sho did it well;
Y'all made my woman dumb as hell.
Dis kinda strife y'all didn't think I know,
'Cause y'all don't even know that my name is Mose.

You think I believe you go to church to serve the Lord,
But I know most of you don't believe in nothing at all.
Just one hour on Sunday so you can clear your conscience,
Then ya start to serve till next Sunday your God called money.
I been figurin' this out and I did it pretty well,
But I tell ya it took me a long time and I'm tired.
How tired I am y'all don't know
'Cause y'all don't know that my name is Mose.

Y'all don't see me walking that line
With most of my own folks out of their mind.
If they ain't hung up on religion and the lack,
They mad at the world 'cause they're black,
Or thinking their color make them better than anyone,
Not facing the fact that cha can be a black or white dum-dum.
But how in the hell y'all gonna know?
Y'all don't even know that my name is Mose.

Y'all can't feel that spirit in my neighborhood,
See that's an evil spirit and Lord knows that ain't good.
Now we done start judging people by the color of their skin,
We even turned on the few white folks that stuck around to prove
     they're friends.
Y'all do know every word is true
And you're too damn dumb to know what to do,
Ya say ya so smart but it still don't show
'Cause y'all don't even know that my name is Mose.

Y'all can't see the young ain't listenin' to the old
And they can't lead themselves 'cause they don't know where to go,
So they follow the one who give them someone to blame
And make that leader rich and they stay dumb and poor just the same.
I could get rich by foolin' the people; leaders are doin' that ya know,
But that ain't the way, that ain't the way I wanna go.
I could straighten this mess out but y'all don't know
'Cause y'all don't even know that my name is Mose.

I can't get time on your radio and television
To help them young ones learn to make real good decisions,
I don't guess y'all can see too far,
Or would my doing good make me a star?
Here's one thing should be understood:
It's bad when any person or group think they got a monopoly on good.
I could help us a lot but y'all don't know,
Y'all still don't know my name is Mose.

Now back ta us—if we so full of hate for the man,
Why don't we give him back his jobs and make it with your own
*   brains and hands?*
Say you hate 'em 'cause it's true, the system treats you wrong,
But we're lying to ourselves 'cause deep down inside we know
We ain't got no individual system of our own.
Or go on what our forefathers left and that ain't much,
Their biggest business has always been a hallalujah church.
How can you think free when you ain't been free before?
Y'all ain't even learned my name is Mose.

To survive y'all made me build myself a radar mind
And even from the sound of your voice I kin tell you're lying,
Like y'all don't mind me havin' your daughter all my life—
If it's the one by your black woman and not by your white wife.
I bet you say no integration to your daughter and son,
But why don't y'all tell 'em 'bout back in slavery where mulattos come from?
I bet y'all thought da women folk should never know
Just t'ow got cheated her and old Mose.

Y'all think I'm mad for you doing all that,
But you didn't make a mule to fight you back,
Ain't I the damndest thing you ever seen,
Being treated like a mule but turn out to be a human being?
I feel and care for more than just mine,
And I laugh with·a burden that would have others cryin',
And what da hell y'all don't know,
Y'all don't even known that my name is Mose.

My Neighborhood

Words and Music by John W. Anderson
KaSandra, Capitol 2957

Newspapers, beer cans and broken glass,
Garbage that smells fumes up the main drag;
The educated got jobs while the laborers lag–
From the corner they yak about what ain't their bag.
Papa stoppa sendin' soda bottles all the time,
We wouldn't last half a day without a short neck of wine.
Leroy smokin' roches got caught and had to pay,
The judge just give him a year and a day.

Tommy he's frontin' for the liquor store again,
He ain't had a raise since I don't know when.
Grocery store Willie can't say one word,
The pawnbroker'll get him fired, least that's what I heard.
What's the police doin' searchin' poor deacon Jones
When the bank just got robbed they know the robbers are gone?
It ain't gettin' no better so I'm gonna split,
I was born in this dump but Lord I ain't glued to it.

This is my home–how you like where I was born?
If you like it you stay, I'm on my way,
So help me today I'm gone.

They killed brother Lucas for non-support,
No job, no lawyer, he had a kangaroo court.
From the poverty people no poverty funds,
It was all used up on the higher echelons.
Preacher man gettin' a kick back from the politicians downtown–
The members got hip but too scared to put him down.
Lord I want to tell you this is no place for me,
Got to find that good life that I see on T.V.

This is my home–now how you like where I was born?
If you like it you stay, I'm on my way,
So help me today I'm gone.

An Elementary School Class Room in a Slum

Stephen Spender

Far far from gusty waves, these children's faces.
Like rootless weeds the torn hair round their pallor.
The tall girl with her weighed-down head. The paper-seeming boy with
    rat's eyes. The stunted unlucky heir
Of twisted bones, reciting a father's gnarled disease,
His lesson from his desk. At back of the dim class
One unnoted, sweet and young. His eyes live in a dream
Of squirrels' game, in tree room, other than this.

On sour cream walls, donations. Shakespeare's head,
Cloudless at dawn, civilized dome riding all cities.
Belled, flowery, Tyrolese valley. Open-handed map
Awarding the world its world. And yet, for these
Children, these windows, not this world, are world,
Where all their future's painted with a fog,
A narrow street sealed in with a lead sky,
Far far from rivers, capes, and stars of words.

Surely, Shakespeare is wicked, the map a bad example
With ships and sun and love tempting them to steal—
For lives that slyly turn in their cramped holes
From fog to endless night? On their slag heap, these children
Wear skins peeped through by bones and spectacles of steel
With mended glass, like bottle bits on stones.
All of their time and space are foggy slum
So blot their maps with slums as big as doom.

Unless, governor, teacher, inspector, visitor,
This map becomes their window and these windows
That shut upon their lives like crouching tombs
Break, O break open, till they break the town
And show the children to green fields and make their world
Run azure on sold sands, to let their tongues
Run naked into books, the white and green leaves open
History theirs whose language is the sun.

from

London

Samuel Johnson

By numbers here from shame or censure free
All crimes are safe, but hated poverty.
This, only this, the rigid law pursues;
This, only this, provokes the snarling muse.
The sober trader at a tatter'd cloak
Wakes from his dream, and labours for a joke;
With brisker air the silken courtiers gaze,
And turn the varied taunt a thousand ways,
Of all the griefs that harass the distress'd,
Sure the most bitter is a scornful jest;
Fate never wounds more deep the gen'rous heart,
Than when a blockhead's insult points the dart.
Has heaven reserv'd, in pity to the poor,
No pathless waste, or undiscover'd shore?
No secret island in the boundless main?
No peaceful desert yet unclaim'd by Spain?
Quick let us rise, the happy seats explore,
And bear oppression's insolence no more.
This mournful truth is ev'ry where confess'd,
SLOW RISES WORTH, BY POVERTY DEPRESS'D:
But here more slow, where all are slaves to gold,
Where looks are merchandise, and smiles are sold;
Where won by bribes, by flatteries implor'd,
The groom retails the favours of his lord.

Holy Thursday

from
Songs of Experience

William Blake

Is this a holy thing to see
In a rich and fruitful land,
Babes reduc'd to misery,
Fed with cold and usurous hand?

Is that trembling cry a song?
Can it be a song of joy?
And so many children poor?
It is a land of poverty!

And their sun does never shine,
And their fields are bleak & bare,
And their ways are fill'd with thorns:
It is eternal winter there.

For where-e'er the sun does shine,
And where-e'er the rain does fall,
Babe can never hunger there,
Nor poverty the mind appall.

Don't Pat Me on the Back and Call Me Brother

Words and Music by John W. Anderson
KaSandra, Capitol ST 2957

Spoken:

We who ain't got no respect for each other—
If I'm good in one thing I don't respect you for being good in another—
If your money is a little bit longer than mine,
Right away you want to disrespect me and treat me unkind.
So until we learn to respect each other,
Don't pat me on the back and call me brother.

Y'see we think ain't nobody got no sense but us,
And we're somethin' special 'cause we happened to get out of touch.
We'll help each other git just a wee little bit,
But if I think you're gonna make it—baby that's it.
So until we learn to really help each other,
Don't pat me on the back and call me your brother.

Y'all been tellin' me who will cheat me, saying he's a devil and cruel as
*   can be,*
But the biggest cheating I ever got a brother gave it to me.
We think we are all honest enough—
It's alright to tell the truth but not on us—
We look at the faults in everybody else,
That's why we can't see what's wrong with ourselves.
So until we start being honest with each other,
Remember your daddy ain't my daddy and my mother ain't your mother.
So don't be patting me on my back, trying to put your hand in my pocket,
By callin' me your cotton pickin' brother.

Just Look in my Face

Words and Music by John W. Anderson
KaSandra, Capitol ST 2957

I'm a cotton field in the burning sun,
I'm a lash of a whip, Lord, when the day is done,
I'm a mother takin' my son
From the end of a rope; and what he's done
Even God don't know.

And the pain my mama felt while she was breakin' that corn
'Cause the boss made her work, Lord, till the hour I was born;
These are the hands that fix this food with a smile,
And in my mama's lap she rocked the boss's child.
Tell me now, do you want to see this land?
Well you come on and take a look at this place.
Tell me now, do you want to see this land?
Well all you gotta do is look, look, look, look in my face.

I'm a man on a battlefield far away from home
Fightin' for somethin' I've never known.
Echoes from the past guide me from day to day
And to know I'm goin' right keeps me on my way.

I Am

John Clare

I am: yet what I am none cares or knows,
   My friends forsake me like a memory lost,
I am the self-consumer of my woes–
   They rise and vanish in oblivious host,
Like shadows in love's frenzied stifled throes–
And yet I am, and live–like vapors tossed

Into the nothingness of scorn and noise,
   Into the living sea of waking dreams,
Where there is neither sense of life or joys,
   But the vast shipwreck of my life's esteems;
And e'en the dearest, that I love the best,
Are strange–nay, rather stranger than the rest.

I long for scenes, where man hath never trod,
   A place where woman never smiled or wept–
There to abide with my Creator, God,
   And sleep as I in childhood sweetly slept,
Untroubling, and untroubled where I lie,
The grass below–above the vaulted sky.

3

Woody Guthrie

In early Christian times, Christians enjoyed communion with one another by taking their meals in common. Each meal was an "agape," the Greek word for "love feast," and they would share it not only among themselves but also with anyone who was in need, for Jesus had said; "when thou makest a feast, call the poor, the maimed, the lame, the blind [Luke 14:13]." Recalling this practice, the term "agape" now suggests active concern for one's fellow man, especially the common, ordinary man struggling to make his way through this world. Woody Guthrie, Ewan MacColl, Phil Ochs, and Jacques Brel—the songwriters considered in these opening chapters—might well be considered to express, in their different ways, this kind of social awareness.

Woody Guthrie (1912-1967) is today generally regarded as the finest of the traditional folk song composers whose names are known to us. He is the spiritual and musical godfather to Bob Dylan, Phil Ochs, Eric Anderson, and in fact, all the leading songwriters of the past decade whose roots are in the American folk song tradition. During his lifetime, however, recognition came to him only in his final years after a crippling disease permanently hospitalized him. The renowned literary and musical critic, Clifton Fadiman, called Guthrie "one of America's great natural resources".

The two ballads in this section—*Hard Travelin'* and
Tom Joad—represent the special qualities of his work—
passionate simplicity edged by wry humor, oneness with
the life of working people, and an ability to uncover the
poetry of rough, common speech. Guthrie wrote *Tom Joad*
after seeing the film version of John Steinbeck's great
novel of the 1930's, *The Grapes of Wrath.* The result is a
perfect example of the narrative folk ballad that evokes a
complex and highly charged situation by means of
presenting only the essence of what happens. The one
difference is that in *Tom Joad,* the traditionally impersonal
and objective narrator is replaced by a speaker who is
totally involved with his story—a change that in this case
seems to be all to the good since it adds the appeal of
Guthrie's intense humanity.

Tom Joad

Words and Music by Woody Guthrie
Dust Bowl Ballads, Folkways FH 5212

Tom Joad got out of that old McAlester Pen,
It was there that he got his parole
After four long years on a man killing charge,
Tom Joad come a walking down the road. Poor boy.
Tom Joad come a walking down the road.

It was there that he found him a truck driving man,
It was there that he caught him a ride,
Said "I just got a loose from McAlester's pen
On a charge called homicide. Great God.
A charge called homicide."

That truck rolled away in a big cloud of dust
And Tommy turned his face towards home,
He met Preacher Casey and they had a little drink
And he found that his family they was gone. Tom Joad.
He found that his family they was gone.

He found his mother's old fashion shoe
And he found his daddy's hat,
He found Little Muley and Little Muley said,
"They been tractored out by th' cats. Tom.
They been tractored out by th' cats."

Well Tom he walked over to the neighboring farm
And he found his family
And they took Preacher Casey and they loaded in a car
And his mammy said "we got to git away Tom."
His mammy said "we got to get away."

The twelve of the Joads made a might heavy load
And Grandpa Joad he cried,
He picked up a handful of land in his hand
And said "I'm stickin' with my farm till I die.
I'm stickin' with my farm till I die."

They fed him spare ribs and coffee and soothing syrup
And Grandpa Joad he died.
We buried Grandpa Joad on the Oklahoma road
And Grandma on the California side,
And Grandma on the California side.

We stood on a mountain and we looked to the west
And it looked like the promised land,
Was a big green valley with a river running through
And there was work for every single hand. We thought.
There was work for every single hand.

Now the Joads rolled into a jungle camp,
It was there that they cooked them a stew,
And the hungry little kids in the jungle camp
Said "We'd like to have some too. Yes.
We'd like to have some too."

A deputy sheriff fired loose at a man
And he shot a woman in the back,
But before he could take his aim again
It was Preacher Casey dropped him in his tracks. Good boy.
Preacher Casey dropped him in his tracks.

Well they handcuffed Casey and they took him to jail,
And then he got away,
And he met Tom Joad by the old river bridge
And these few words he did say. Preacher Casey.
These few words he did say.

Well I preached for the Lord a mighty long time.
I preached about the rich and the poor.
But us workin' folks has got to stick together
Or we ain't got a chance anymore. God knows.
We ain't got a chance any more.

Then the deputies come and Tom and Casey run
To a place where the water run down,
And a vigilante thug hit Casey with a club
And he laid Preacher Casey on the ground.
And he laid Preacher Casey on the ground.

Tom Joad he grabbed that deputy's club
And he brung it down on his head,
When Tommy took flight that dark and rainy night
Was a preacher and a deputy lying dead. Two men.
A preacher and a deputy lying dead.

Tommy run back where his mama was asleep
And he woke her up out of bed,
And he kissed goodbye to the mother that he loved
And he said what Preacher Casey said. Tom Joad.
He said what Preacher Casey said.

Ever'body might be just one big soul,
Well it looks that a way to me,
So everywhere you look in the day or the night
That's where I'm gonna be, Ma.
That's where I'm gonna be.

Wherever little kids are hungry and cry,
Wherever people ain't free,
Wherever men are fightin' for their rights,
That's where I'm gonna be, Ma.
That's where I'm gonna be.

Frederick Douglass

Robert Hayden

When it is finally ours, this freedom, this liberty,
       this beautiful
and terrible thing, needful to man as air,
usable as earth; when it belongs at last to all,
when it is truly instinct, brain matter, diastole, systole,
reflex action; when it is finally won; when it is more
than the gaudy mumbo jumbo of politicians:
this man, this Douglass, this former slave, this Negro
beaten to his knees, exiled, visioning a world
where none is lonely, none hunted, alien,
this man, superb in love and logic, this man
shall be remembered, Oh, not with statues' rhetoric,
not with legends and poems and wreaths of bronze alone,
but with the lives grown out of his life, the lives
fleshing his dream of the beautiful needful thing.

I Think Continually

Stephen Spender

I think continually of those who were truly great.
Who, from the womb, remembered the soul's history
Through corridors of light where the hours are suns,
Endless and singing. Whose lovely ambition
Was that their lips, still touched with fire,
Should tell of the Spirit clothed from head to foot in song.
And who hoarded from the Spring branches
The desires falling across their bodies like blossoms.

What is precious is never to forget
The essential delight of the blood drawn from ageless
    springs
Breaking through rocks in worlds before our earth.
Never to deny its pleasure in the simple morning light
Nor its grave evening demand for love.
Never to allow gradually the traffic to smother
With noise and fog the flowering of the Spirit.

Near the snow, near the sun, in the highest fields,
See how these names are feted by the wavering grass
And by the streamers of white cloud
And whispers of wind in the listening sky.
The names of those who in their lives fought for life,
Who wore at their hearts the fire's centre.
Born of the sun, they travelled a short while towards the sun,
And left the vivid air signed with their honour.

from
The Deserted Village

Oliver Goldsmith

Ill fares the land, to hastening ills a prey,
Where wealth accumulates and men decay;
Princes and lords may flourish or may fade;
A breath can make them as a breath has made:
But a bold peasantry, their country's pride,
When once destroyed, can never be supplied.
   A time there was, ere England's griefs began,
When every rood of ground maintained its man;
For him light labour spread her wholesome store,
Just gave what life required, but gave no more:
His best companions, innocence and health;
And his best riches, ignorance of wealth.
   But times are altered; trade's unfeeling train
Usurp the land, and dispossess the swain;
Along the lawn, where scattered hamlets rose,
Unwieldy wealth and cumbrous pomp repose;
And every want to opulence allied,
And every pang that folly pays to pride.
Those gentle hours that plenty bade to bloom,
Those calm desires that asked but little room,
Those helpful sports that graced the peaceful scene,
Lived in each look, and brightened all the green—
These, far departing, seek a kinder shore,
And rural mirth and manners are no more.

                • • •

   Yes! let the rich deride, the proud disdain,
These simple blessings of the lowly train;
To me more dear, congenial to my heart,
One native charm, than all the gloss of art;
Spontaneous joys, where nature has its play,
The soul adopts, and owns their first-born sway;
Lightly they frolic o'er the vacant mind,
Unenvied, unmolested, unconfined.
But the long pomp, the midnight masquerade,
With all the freaks of wanton wealth arrayed,–
In these, ere triflers half their wish obtain,
The toiling pleasure sicknes into pain;
And e'en while fashion's brightest arts decoy,
The heart distrusting asks if this be joy.

Ye friends to truth, ye statesmen, who survey
The rich man's joy increase, the poor's decay,
'Tis yours to judge how wide the limits stand
Between a splendid and an happy land.
Proud swells the tide with loads of freighted ore,
And shouting Folly hails them from her shore;
Hoards even beyond the miser's wish abound,
And rich men flock from all the world around.
Yet count our gains: this wealth is but a name
That leaves our useful products still the same.
Not so the loss: the man of wealth and pride
Takes up a space that many poor supplied;
Space for his lake, his park's extended bounds,
Space for his horse, equipage, and hounds;
The robe that wraps his limbs in silken sloth
Has robbed the neighbouring fields of half their growth;
His seat, where solitary sports are seen,
Indignant spurns the cottage from the green;
Around the world each needful product flies,
For all the luxuries the world supplies;
While thus the land, adorned for pleasure all,
In barren splendor feebly waits the fall.
       • • •
Where then, ah where, shall poverty reside,
To 'scape the pressure of contiguous pride?
If to some common's fenceless limits strayed,
He drives his flock to pick the scanty blade,
Those fenceless fields the sons of wealth divide,
And even the bare-worn common is denied.
    If to the city sped—what waits him there?
To see profusion that he must not share;
To see ten thousand baneful arts combined
To pamper luxury, and thin mankind;
To see those joys the sons of pleasure know
Extorted from his fellow-creature's woe.
Here while the courtier glitters in brocade,
There the pale artist plies the sickly trade;
Here while the proud their long-drawn pomps display,
There the black gibbet glooms beside the way;
The dome where Pleasure holds her midnight reign,
Here, richly decked, admits the gorgeous train;
Tumultuous grandeur crowds the blazing square,
The rattling chariots clash, the torches glare.

Sure scenes like these no troubles e'er annoy!
Sure these denote one universal joy!
Are these thy serious thoughts?–Ah, turn thine eyes
Where the poor houseless shivering female lies.
She once, perhaps, in village plenty blessed,
Has wept at tales of innocence distressed;
Her modest looks the cottage might adorn,
Sweet as the primrose peeps beneath the thorn;
Now lost to all–her friends, her virtue fled–
Near her betrayer's door she lays her head,
And, pinched with cold, and shrinking from the shower,
With heavy heart deplores that luckless hour,
When idly first, ambitious of the town,
She left her wheel and robes of country brown.

• • •

Good Heaven! what sorrows gloomed that parting day
That called them from their native walks away;
When the poor exiles, every pleasure past,
Hung round their bowers, and fondly looked their last,
And took a long farewell, and wished in vain
For seats like these beyond the western main;
And, shuddering still to face the distant deep,
Returned and wept, and still returned to weep.
The good old sire the first prepared to go
To new-found worlds, and wept for others' woe;
But for himself, in conscious virtue brave,
He only wished for worlds beyond the grave.
His lovely daughter, lovelier in her tears,
The found companion of his helpless years,
Silent went next, neglectful of her charms,
And left a lover's for a father's arms.
With louder plaints the mother spoke her woes,
And blessed the cot where every pleasure rose,
And kissed her thoughtless babes with many a tear,
And clasped them close, in sorrow doubly dear;
Whilst her fond husband strove to lend relief
In all the silent manliness of grief.

O Luxury! thou cursed by Heaven's decree,
How ill exchanged are things like these for thee!
How do thy potions, with insidious joy,
Diffuse their pleasure only to destroy!
Kingdoms by thee, to sickly greatness grown,
Boast of a florid vigour not their own:
At every draught more large and large they grow,
A bloated mass of rank, unwieldy woe;
Till, sapped their strength, and every part unsound,
Down, down they sink, and spread a ruin round.

     • • •

Hard Travelin'

Words and Music by Woody Guthrie
Woody Guthrie, Folkways FA 2483

I've been doing some hard traveling, I thought you knowed,
I've been doing some hard rambling, way down the road,
For I've been doing some hard rambling, hard drinking, hard gambling,
I've been doing some hard traveling, Lord.

I've been doing some hardrock mining, I thought you knowed,
I've been leaning on a pressure drill, way down the road,
Well, the hammer flying and the air hose sucking,
And six feet of mud and I sure been a-mucking,
And I've been doing some hard traveling, Lord.

I've been laying in a hard rock jail, I thought you knowed, boys,
I've been laying out ninety days, way down the road,
Well, the darned old judge he said to me,
It's ninety days for vagrancy,
And I've been doing some hard traveling, Lord.

I've been riding them fast passengers, I thought you knowed, boys,
I've been hitting them flat wheelers, way down the road,
I've been riding them blind passengers,
Dead enders, kicking up cinders,
I've been doing some hard traveling, Lord.

I've been doing some hard harvesting, I thought you knowed,
From North Dakota to Kansas City, way down the road,
Been a-cutting that wheat and a-stacking that hay,
Just trying to make about a dollar a day,
And I've been doing some hard harvesting, Lord.

I've been walking that Lincoln Highway, I thought you knowed,
I've been hitting that '66 way down the road,
Got a heavy load, I got a worried mind,
I'm looking for a woman that's hard to find,
And I've been doing some hard traveling, Lord.

nobody loses all the time

E. E. Cummings

nobody loses all the time

i had an uncle named
Sol who was a born failure and
nearly everybody said he should have gone
into vaudeville perhaps because my Uncle Sol could
sing McCann He Was A Diver on Xmas Eve like Hell Itself which
may or may not account for the fact that my Uncle

Sol indulged in that possibly most inexcusable
of all to use a highfalootin phrase
luxuries that is or to
wit farming and be
it needlessly
added

my Uncle Sol's farm
failed because the chickens
ate the vegetables so
my Uncle Sol had a
chicken farm till the
skunks ate the chickens when

my Uncle Sol
had a skunk farm but
the skunks caught cold and
died and so
my Uncle Sol imitated the
skunks in a subtle manner

or by drowning himself in the watertank
but somebody who'd given my Uncle Sol a Victor
Victrola and records while he lived presented to
him upon the auspicious occasion of his decease a
scrumptious not to mention splendiferous funeral with
tall boys in back gloves and flowers and everything and

i remember we all cried like the Missouri
when my Uncle Sol's coffin lurched because
somebody pressed a button
(and down went
my Uncle
Sol

and started a worm farm)

The Southern Road

Dudley Randall

There the black river, boundary to hell,
And here the iron bridge, the ancient car,
And grim conductor, who with surly yell
Forbids white soldiers where the black ones are.
And I re-live the enforced avatar
Of desparate journey to a dark abode
Made by my sires before another war;
And I set forth upon the southern road.

To a land where shadowed songs like flowers swell
And where the earth is scarlet as a scar
Friezed by the bleeding lash that fell (O fell!)
Upon my fathers' flesh. O far, far, far
And deep my blood has drenched it. None can bar
My birthright to the loveliness bestowed
Upon this country haughty as a star.
And I set forth upon the southern road.

This darkness and these mountains loom a spell
Of peak-roofed town where yearning steeples soar
And the holy holy chanting of a bell
Shakes human incense on the throbbing air
Where bonfires blaze and quivering bodies char.
Whose is the hair that crisped, and fiercely glowed?
I know it; and my entrails melt like tar
And I set forth upon the southern road.

O fertile hillsides where my fathers are,
And whence my woes like troubled streams have flowed,
Love you I must, though they may sweep me far.
And I set forth upon the southern road.

from

Song of the Open Road

Walt Whitman

Afoot and light-hearted I take to the open road,
Healthy, free, the world before me,
The long brown path before me leading wherever I choose.
Henceforth I ask not good-fortune, I myself am good-fortune,
Henceforth I whimper no more, postpone no more, need nothing,
Done with indoor complaints, libraries, querulous criticisms,
Strong and content I travel the open road.
The earth, that is sufficient,
I do not want the constellations any nearer,
I know they are very well where they are,
I know they suffice for those who belong to them.

(Still here I carry my old delicious burdens,
I carry them, men and women, I carry them with me wherever I go,
I swear it is impossible for me to get rid of them,
I am fill'd with them; and I will fill them in return.)
      • • •
Listen! I will be honest with you,
I do not offer the old smooth prizes, but offer rough new prizes,
These are the days that must happen to you:
You shall not heap up what is call'd riches,
You shall scatter with lavish hand all that you earn or achieve,
You but arrive at the city to which you were destin'd, you
    hardly settle yourself to satisfaction before you are call'd
    by an irresistible call to depart,
You shall be treated to the ironical smiles and mockings of
    those who remain behind you,
What beckonings of love you receive you shall only answer
    with passionate kisses of parting,
You shall not allow the hold of those who spread their reach'd
    hands toward you.
      • • •

All parts away for the progress of souls,
All religion, all solid things, arts, governments–all that was or is
    apparent upon this globe or any globe, falls into niches and corners before
    the procession of souls along the grand roads of the universe.
Of the progress of the souls of men and women along the grand roads
    of the universe, all other progress is the needed emblem and sustenance.
Forever alive, forever forward,
Stately, solemn, sad, withdrawn, baffled, mad, turbulent,
    feeble, dissatisfied,
Desperate, proud, fond, sick, accepted by men, rejected by men,
They go! they go! I know that they go, but I know not where they go,
But I know that they go toward the best–toward something great.

Whoever you are, come forth! or man or woman come forth!
You must not stay sleeping and dallying there in the house,
    though you built it, or though it has been built for you.

Out of the dark confinement! out from behind the screen!
It is useless to protest. I know all and expose it.
Behold through you as bad as the rest,
Through the laughter, dancing, dining, supping, of people,
Inside of dresses and ornaments, inside of those wash'd and
    trimm'd faces,
Behold a secret silent loathing and despair.

No husband, no wife, no friend, trusted to hear the confession,
Another self, a duplicate of every one, skulking and hiding it goes,
Formless and wordless through the streets of the cities, polite
    and bland in the parlors,
In the cars of railroads, in steamboats, in the public assembly,
Home to the houses of men and women, at the table, in the
    bedroom, everywhere,
Smartly attired, countenance smiling, form upright, death
    under the breast-bones, hell under the skull-bones,
Under the broadcloth and gloves, under the ribbons and artificial flowers,
Keeping fair with the customs, speaking not a syllable of itself,
Speaking of any thing else but never of itself.

Let the tools remain in the workshop! let the money remain unearn'd!
Let the school stand! mind not the cry of the teacher!
Let the preacher preach in his pulpit! let the lawyer plead in
    the court, and the judge expound the law.
Camerado, I give you my hand!
I give you my love more precious than money,
I give you myself before preaching or law;
Will you give me yourself? will you come travel with me?
Shall we stick by each other as long as we live?

4

Ewan MacColl

In both North America and Great Britain, a primary source
of nourishment for the present revolution in popular song
was folk music. The traditions of folk music were kept alive
in North America by such singer-writers as Pete Seeger
and Woody Guthrie, who used folk idioms to express
thoughts and feelings relevant to contemporary life—
especially the aspects that old-style commercial
songwriters wouldn't dare talk about. In Great Britain, a
similar service was performed by such singer-composers
as Ewan MacColl, whose work is represented in this section.

It might be useful to compare MacColl's folk song, *The
Ballad of the Carpenter,* with Guthrie's *Tom Joad.* MacColl's
power as an artful composer is shown in *The First Time
Ever I Saw Your Face.* It would be hard to find a ballad
that expresses honest, sexual love more beautifully.

The Ballad of the Carpenter

Words and Music by Ewan MacColl
New Britain Gazette (1), Folkways FW 8732

*Jesus was a working man, a hero you
        shall hear,
Born in the slums of Bethlehem, at the
        turning of the year,
Yes, the turning of the year.*

*When Jesus was a little boy, the streets
        rang with his name,
For he argued with the alderman and he
        put 'em all to shame,
Yes, he put them all to shame.*

*His father he apprenticed him a carpenter
        to be.
To plane and drill and work with skill in
        the town of Galilee,
Yes, the town of Galilee.*

*He became a roving journeyman and he
        wandered far and wide,
And he saw how wealth and poverty live
        always side by side,
Yes, always side by side.*

*He said, "Come all you working men, you
        farmers and weavers, too—
If you will only organize the world belongs
        to you,
Yes, the world belongs to you."*

*So the fishermen sent two delegates and the
        farmers and weavers too,
And they formed a working committee of
        twelve to see the struggle through,
Yes, to see the struggle through.*

*When the rich men heard what the carpenter
        had done, to the Roman troops they ran,
Saying, "Put this rebel, Jesus, down, he's
        a menace to God and man,
Yes, a menace to God and man."*

The commander of the occupying troops,
he laughed and then he said,
"There's a cross to spare on Calvary Hill,
by the weekend he'll be dead,
Yes, by the weekend, he'll be dead."

Now, Jesus walked among the poor, for
the poor were his own kind,
And they wouldn't let the cops get near
enough to take him from behind,
Yes, to take him from behind.

So they hired a man of the traitor's trade,
and a stool pigeon was he.
And he sold his brother to the butcher's
men for a fistful of silver money,
A fistful of money.

When Jesus lay in the prison cell, they
beat him and offered him bribes,
To desert the cause of his own poor folk
and work for the rich men's tribe,
Yes, to work for the rich men's tribe.

The sweat stood out upon his brow, and the
blood was in his eye,
And they nailed his body to the Roman Cross
and they laughed as they watched him die,
Yes, they laughed as they watched him die.

Two thousand years have passed and gone,
and many a hero, too,
And the dream of this poor carpenter, at
last it's coming true.
Yes, at last it's coming true.

For Easter-Day

Charles Wesley

"Christ the Lord is risen to-day,"
Sons of men and angels say.
Raise your joys and triumphs high;
Sing, ye heavens, and earth reply.

Love's redeeming work is done,
Fought the fight, the battle won.
Lo! our Sun's eclipse is o'er;
Lo! He sets in blood no more.

Vain the stone, the watch, the seal;
Christ has burst the gates of hell!
Death in vain forbids His rise:
Christ has opened Paradise.

Lives again our glorious King;
Where, O Death, is now thy sting?
Dying once, He all doth save;
Where thy victory, O Grave?

Soar we now where Christ has led,
Following our exalted Head:
Made like Him, like Him we rise;
Ours the Cross, the grave, the skies!

What though once we perished all,
Partners in our parents' fall:
Second life we all receive,
In our heavenly Adam live.

Risen with Him, we upward move,
Still we seek the things above,
Still pursue, and kiss the Son,
Seated on His Father's throne.

Scarce on earth a thought bestow;
Dead to all we leave below:
Heaven our aim, and loved abode,
Hid our life with Christ in God.

Hid, till Christ our Life appear,
Glorious in His members here:
Joined to Him, we then shall shine
All immortal, all divine.

Hail, the Lord of earth and heaven!
Praise to Thee by both be given:
Thee we greet triumphant now;
Hail, the Resurrection Thou!

King of glory, Soul of bliss,
Everlasting life is this,
Thee to know, Thy power to prove,
Thus to sing, and thus to love.

The First Time Ever I Saw Your Face

Words and Music by Ewan MacColl
New Britain Gazette (2), Folkways FW 8734

The first time ever I saw your face
I thought the sun rose in your eyes,
And the moon and stars were the gift you gave
To the dark and empty skies, my love,
To the dark and empty skies.

The first time ever I kissed your mouth,
I felt the earth move in my hand,
Like the trembling heart of a captive bird
That was there at my command, my love,
That was there at my command.

The first time ever I lay with you
And felt your heartbeat close to mine,
I thought our joy would fill the earth
And last till the end of time, my love,
And last till the end of time.

Who Ever Loved, That Loved Not at First Sight?

from
Hero and Leander

Chirstopher Marlowe

It lies not in our power to love or hate,
For will in us is overruled by fate.
When two are stripped, long ere the course begin,
We wish that one should lose, the other win;
And one especially do we affect
Of two gold ingots, like in each respect:
The reason no man knows; let it suffice
What we behold is censured by our eyes.
Where both deliberate, the love is slight:
Who ever loved, that loved not at first sight?

But, Soft! What Light Through Yonder Window Breaks?

William Shakespeare
(Romeo and Juliet, Act II, Scene 2)

But, soft! what light through yonder window breaks
It is the east, and Juliet is the sun!
Arise, fair sun, and kill the envious moon,
Who is already sick and pale with grief,
That thou her maid art far more fair than she:
Be not her maid, since she is envious;
Her vestal livery is but sick and green,
And none but fools do wear it; cast it off.
It is my lady; O! it is my love:
O! that she knew she were.
She speaks, yet she says nothing: what of that
Her eye discourses; I will answer it.
I am too bold, 'tis not to me she speaks:
Two of the fairest stars in all the heaven,
Having some business, do entreat her eyes
To twinkle in their spheres till they return.
What if her eyes were there, they in her head?
The brightness of her cheek would shame those stars
As daylight doth a lamp; her eyes in heaven
Would through the airy region stream so bright
That birds would sing and think it were not night.
See! how she leans her cheek upon her hand:
O! that I were a glove upon that hand,
That I might touch that cheek.

5

Phil Ochs

Phil Ochs is one of the most heavily criticized
New Generation songwriters.
One reason he troubles his critics so much is that his
songs are mercilessly unrelenting, forcing us to consider
man's inhumanity to man in detail after detail.

Another reason is that people continue to buy his records
and attend his concerts, despite—or perhaps even
because of—this assumed fault. And Ochs' following
continues to grow, notwithstanding the reluctance of
American TV and radio stations to broadcast his
controversial material.

The Crucifixion is one of the best examples of Ochs' songs.
Occasioned by the assasination of President Kennedy,
it reaches beyond this event into the well-springs of evil,
and what it finds there, Ochs can express only in highly
metaphorical and mystical terms.

Crucifixion

Words and Music by Phil Ochs
Pleasures of the Harbor, A & M 4133

An the night comes again to the circle studded sky,
The stars settle slowly, in loneliness they lie.
Till the universe explodes as a falling star is raised,
The planets are paralyzed; the mountains are amazed;
But they all glow brighter from the brillance of the blaze,
With the speed of insanity, then he dies!

In the green fields of turning, a baby is born;
His cries crease the wind, and mingle with the morn,
An assault upon the order, the changing of the guard,
Chosen for a challenge that's hopelessly hard,
And the only single sign is the sighing of the stars;
But to the silence of distance, they're sworn!

   Chorus:

So Dance, Dance, Dance;
teach us to be true.
Come Dance, Dance, Dance;
'cause we love you.

Images of innocence charge him to go on,
But the decadence of history is looking for a pawn,
To a nightmare of knowledge he opens up the gate;
A blinding revelation is served upon his plate,
That beneath the greatest love is a hurricane of hate,
And God help the critic of the dawn.

So he stands on the sea, and he shouts to the shore,
But the louder that he screams, the longer he's ignored.
For the wine of oblivion is drunk to the dregs,
And the merchants of the masses almost have to be begged
Till the giant is aware that someone's pulling at his leg,
And someone is tapping at the door.

   Chorus

Then his message gathers meaning, and it spreads across the land,
The rewarding of the fame is the following of the man,
But ignorance is everywhere and people have their way,
And success is an enemy to the losers of the day.
In the shadows of the churches who knows what they pray.
And blood is the language of the band.

The Spanish bulls are beaten; the crowd is soon beguiled,
The matador is beautiful, a symphony of style.
Excitement is ecstatic; passion places bets.
Gracefully he bows to ovations that he gets;
But the hands that are applauding are slippery with sweat,
And saliva is falling from their smiles.

Chorus

Then this overflow of life is crushed into a liar,
The gentle soul is ripped apart and tossed into the fire,
It's the burial of beauty; it's the victory of night,
Truth becomes a tragedy limping from the light.
The heavens are horrified; they stagger from the sight,
And the cross is trembling with desire.

They say they can't believe it, "It's a sacrilegious shame.
Now, who would want to hurt such a hero of the game.
But you know I predicted it; I knew he had to fall.
How did it happen? I hope his suffering was small.
Tell me every detail, I've got to know it all,
And do you have a picture of the pain."

Chorus

Time takes her toll, and the memory fades,
But his glory is growing in the magic that he made.
Reality is ruined; there is nothing more to fear.
The drama is distorted to what they want to hear.
Swimming in their sorrow in the twisting of a tear
As they wait for the new thrill parade.

The eyes of the rebel have been branded by the blind.
To the safety of sterility the threat has been refined.
The child was created to the slaughter house he's led.
So good to be alive when the eulogies are read.
The climax of emotion, the worship of the dead
As the cycle of sacrifice unwinds.

And the night comes again to the circle studded sky,
The stars settle slowly, in loneliness they lie.
Till the universe explodes as a falling star is raised,
The planets are paralyzed; the mountains are amazed;
But they all glow brighter from the brilliance of the blaze,
With the speed of insanity, then he dies!

O Captain! My Captain!

Walt Whitman

O Captain! my Captain! our fearful trip is done,
The ship has weather'd every rack, the prize we sought is won,
The port is near, the bells I hear, the people all exulting,
While follow eyes the steady keel, the vessel grim and daring;
      But O heart! heart! heart!
        O the bleeding drops of red,
          Where on the deck my Captain lies,
          Fallen cold and dead.

O Captain! my Captain! rise up and hear the bells;
Rise up–for you the flag is flung–for you the bugle trills,
For you bouquets and ribbon'd wreaths–for you the shores a-crowding,
For you they call, the swaying mass, their eager faces turning;
      Here Captain! dear father!
        The arm beneath your head!
          It is some dream that on the deck,
          You've fallen cold and dead.

My Captain does not answer, his lips are pale and still,
My father does not feel my arm, he has no pulse nor will,
The ship is anchor'd safe and sound, its voyage closed and done,
From fearful trip the victor ship comes in with object won;
      Exult O shores, and ring O bells!
        But I with mournful tread,
          Walk the deck my Captain lies,
          Fallen cold and dead.

from

An Anatomy of the World

John Donne

Then as mankind, so is the world's whole frame
Quite out of joint, almost created lame;
For before God had made up all the rest,
Corruption enter'd and deprav'd the best.
It seiz'd the angels, and then first of all
The world did in her cradle take a fall
And turn'd her brains and took a general maim,
Wringing each joint of th' universal frame.
The noblest part, man, felt it first, and then
Both beasts and plants, curs'd in the curse of man.
So did the world from the first hour decay;
That evening was beginning of the day,
And now the springs and summers which we see,
Like sons of women after fifty be.
And new philosophy calls all in doubt;
The element of fire is quite put out;
The sun is lost, and th' earth, and no man's wit
Can well direct him where to look for it.
And freely men confess that this world's spent,
When in the planets and the firmament
They seek so many new; they see that this
Is crumbled out again to his atomies.
'Tis all in pieces, all coherence gone,
All just supply, and all relation:
Prince, subject, father, son are things forgot,
For every man alone thinks he hath got
To be a phoenix, and that then can be
None of that kind of which he is, but he.

6

David Ackles

Dave Ackles writes from a conservative point of view—
and effectively, too, as evidenced by his song, *His Name Is
Andrew,* a poignant protest against the current "God is
Dead" school of liberal theology.

Students of poetry should pay special attention to the way
he manages narrative technique. Particularly interesting is
his use of emphasis. Why should the focus of each verse
be the line, "His name is Andrew"? That would seem to be
the least significant bit of information in the story. When
we reach the last verse, however, this curiously dispropor-
tionate emphasis is suddenly explained. We see that the
man the narrator has been telling us about is the narrator
himself, and then at once we realize what has been
compelling the singer to unfold his tale: the narrator has
lost his soul and must now regard his former self as
another person whom he can know only by name. The
shift from third to first person at this point also casts the
narrative into a lyric, dramatic framework—another way of
intensifying impact. By simply repeating and then slightly
altering an apparently unimportant tag line, Ackles thus
strengthens considerably the suspense, unity, surprise,
economy, and significance of his narration.

Note the very different fashion in which Matthew Arnold
treats the theme of loss of faith in *Dover Beach.*

His Name Is Andrew

Words and Music by Dave Ackles
Dave Ackles, Electra 74022

1

His name is Andrew,
He works in a canning factory;
He doesn't have a friend,
He chooses to wait alone for his life to end.

When Andrew was just a little boy
He knew all the words to all the hymns of joy,
And he sang them on Sunday
And he sang them on Monday
And in April and in May
And he heard them say,
God is love, God is love,
And he believed them.

2

This child was Andrew,
He lived in a world of innocence,
On him the lion grinned;
He sang in the arms of God as he strummed the wind.

When Andrew was tall and twenty-one,
He wandered from God and wondered what he'd done,
For he still sang on Sunday,
Though he muddled thru' Monday,
With a silence in his head
Till in jest it said,
God redeems, God redeems,
And he believed it.

3
This man was Andrew,
Hearing a voice he thought was stilled;
Back to the arms of grace he stumbled through darkened woods
To a lighted place.

When Andrew returned to love and light,
He lifted his voice and sang away the night;
And the preacher from Sunday
Heard him singing on Monday
And he stopped him with a word.
From the dark, he heard:
God is dead!
God is dead!
And he believed him.

My name is Andrew.
I work in a canning factory.
I do not have a friend.
I choose to wait alone
For this life to end.

A Summer Night

Matthew Arnold

In the deserted moon-blanch'd street
How lonely rings the echo of my feet!
Those windows, which I gaze at, frown,
Silent and white, unopening down,
Repellent as the world;—but see,
A break between the housetops shows
The moon! and, lost behind her, fading dim
Into the dewy dark obscurity
Down at the far horizon's rim,
Doth a whole tract of heaven disclose.
And to my mind the thought
Is on a sudden brought
Of a past night, and a far different scene.

Headlands stood out into the moon-lit deep
As clearly as at noon;
The spring-tide's brimming flow
Heaved dazzlingly between;
Houses with long white sweep
Girdled the glistening bay;
Behind, through the soft air,
The blue haze-cradled mountains spread away.
That night was far more fair—
But the same restless pacings to and fro,
And the same vainly throbbing heart was there,
And the same bright, calm moon.

And the calm moonlight seems to say:
Hast thou then still the old unquiet breast,
Which neither deadens into rest,
Nor ever feels the fiery glow
That whirls the spirit from itself away,
But fluctuates to and fro,
Never by passion quite possess'd
And never quite benumb'd by the world's sway?—
And I, I know not if to pray
Still to be what I am, or yield and be
Like all the other men I see.
For most men in a brazen prison live,
Where in the sun's hot eye,
With heads bent o'er their toil, they languidly
Their lives to some unmeaning taskwork give,
Dreaming of nought beyond their prison wall.
And as, year after year,
Fresh products of their barren labour fall
From their tired hands, and rest
Never yet comes more near,
Gloom settles slowly down over their breast;
And while they try to stem
The waves of mournful thought by which they are prest,
Death in their prison reaches them
Unfreed, having seen nothing, still unblest.

And the rest, a few,
Escape their prison, and depart
On the wide ocean of life anew.
There the freed prisoner, where'er his heart
Listeth, will sail;
Nor does he know how there prevail,
Despotic on that sea,
Trade-winds that cross it from eternity.
Awhile he holds some false way, undebarr'd
By thwarting signs, and braves
The freshening wind and blackening waves.
And then the tempest strikes him; and between
The lightning bursts is seen
Only a driving wreck,
And the pale master on his spar-strewn deck
With anguish'd face and flying hair
Grasping the rudder hard,
Still bent to make some port he knows not where,
Still standing for some false impossible shore.
And sterner comes the roar
Of sea and wind, and through the deepening gloom
Fainter and fainter wreck and helmsman loom,
And he too disappears, and comes no more.

Is there no life, but these alone?
Madman or slave, must man be one?

Plainness and clearness without shadow of stain!
Clearness divine!
Ye heavens, whose pure dark regions have no sign
Of languor, though so calm, and, though so great,
Are yet untroubled and unpassionate;
Who, though so noble, share in the world's toil,
And though so task'd, keep free from dust and soil!
I will not say that your mild deeps retain
A tinge, it may be, of their silent pain
Who have long'd deeply once, and long'd in vain—
But I will rather say that you remain
A world above man's head, to let him see
How boundless might his soul's horizons be,
How vast, yet of what clear transparency!
How it were good to abide there, and breathe free;
How fair a lot to fill
Is left to each man still!

7

Jaques Brel

What is war? The answers depend to some extent on how one views it. Wars may be, for the scholar, the stepping stones of history; for a general, the crucibles of valor; for a social scientist, temporary breakdowns in international communication. Jacques Brel, in his song, *The Dove,* presents an answer from the point of view of a lover. Are all these answers equally valid? Is the truth about war merely a function of different perspectives? Brel compels us to say, No. After hearing his song we seem to discover, suddenly, that of all the ways of viewing war, only the lover's brings us close to its reality.

It might be helpful to know that the speaker of *The Dove* is a French lieutenant watching young recruits board a train on their way to a war in the Congo. *The Dove* is not, however, just a protest against French involvement in the Congo, but a cry against war itself. We can easily imagine the situation described in the song occurring in almost any war. How effective is it? Listen to Judy Collins' rendition and try to recall any English anti-war song that touches us more deeply. And as those who read French can testify, *The Dove* is even more powerful in its original language.

In the French-speaking world, there is a long and highly developed tradition of combining fine poetry and popular song—the tradition of the *chansonnier.* Jacques Brel himself is a leading exponent of this tradition. Prepared by the current revolution in English popular song, England and North America are just beginning to discover him and the riches he represents, particularly because of the successful show, *Jacques Brel is Alive and Well and Living in Paris.* (Hear the Columbia record album of the same name.)

The Dove

Music and French Lyric by Jacques Brel
English Lyric by Alasdair Clayre
Hear Judy Collins, *In My Life*, Electra 74027

Why all these bugles crying
For squads of young men drilled
To kill and to be killed
Stood waiting by this train?
Why the orders loud and hoarse,
Why the engine's groaning cough,
As it strains to drag us off
Into the holocaust?
Why crowds who sing and cry
And shout and fling us flow'rs
And trade their right for ours
To murder and to die?

   Refrain:

   The Dove has torn her wing,
   so no more songs of love.
   We are not here to sing;
   We're here to kill the dove.

Why has this moment come,
When childhood has to die,
When hope shrinks to a sigh
And speech into a drum?
Why are they pale and still
Young boys trained overnight,
Conscripts forced to fight
And dressed in grey to kill?
These rainclouds massing tight,
This trainload battle bound,
This moving burial ground
Sent thund'ring towards the night?

La colombe

Words and Music by Jacques Brel

Pourquoi cette fanfare
Quand les soldats par quatre
Attendent les massacres
Sur le quai d'une gare?
Pourquoi ce train ventru
Qui ronronne et soupire
Avant de nous conduire
Jusqu'au malentendu?
Pourquoi les chants, les cris
Des foul's venues fleurir
Ceux qui ont le droit d'partir
Au nom de leurs conn'ries?

   Refrain:

   Nous n'irons plus au bois,
   la colombe est blessée—
   Nous n'allons pas au bois,
   nous allons la tuer.

Pourquoi l'heur' que voilà
Où finit notre enfance
Où finit notre chance
Où notre train s'en va?
Pourquoi ce lourd convoi
Chargé d'hommes en gris
Repeints-en une nuit
Pour partir en soldats?
Pourquoi ce train de pluie
Pourquoi ce train de guerre
Pourquoi ce cimetière
En marche vers la nuit?

Refrain

Why statues tow'ring brave
Above the last defeat,
Old words and lies repeat
Across the new made grave?
Why the same still birth
That vict'ry always brought,
These hours of glory bought
By men with mouths of earth?
Dead ash without a spark,
Where cities used to be
For guns probe ev'ry light
And crush it into dark?

Refrain

And why your face undone
With jagged lines of tears
That gave in those first years
All peace I ever won?
Your body in the gloom,
The platform fading back
Your shadow on the track
A flower on a tomb?
And why these days ahead,
When I must let you cry
And live prepared to die,
As if our love were dead?

Refrain

Refrain

Pourquoi les monuments
Qu'offriront les défaites,
Les phrases déjà faites
Qui suivront l'enterr'ment?
Pourquoi l'enfant mort né?
Que sera la victoire?
Pourquoi les jours de gloire
Que d'autres auront payés?
Pourquoi ces coins de terre
Que l'on va peindre en gris
Puisque c'est au fusil
Qu'on éteint la lumière?

Refrain

Pourquoi ton cher visage
Dégrafé par les larmes
Qui me rendait les armes
Aux sources du voyage?
Pourquoi ton corps qui sombre
Ton corps qui disparaît
Et n'est plus sur le quai
Qu'une fleur sur un'tombe?
Pourquoi ces prochains jours
Où je devrai penser
A ne plus m'habiller
Que d'un'moitié d'amour?

Refrain

The Send-Off

Wilfred Owen

Down the close, darkening lanes they sang their way
To the siding-shed,
And lined the train with faces grimly gay.
Their breasts were stuck all white with wreath and spray
As men's are, dead.

Dull porters watched them, and a casual tramp
Stood staring hard,
Sorry to miss them from the upland camp.
Then, unmoved, signals nodded, and a lamp
Winked to the guard.

So secretly, like wrongs hushed-up, they went.
They were not ours:
We never heard to which front these were sent.
Nor there if they yet mock what women meant
Who gave them flowers.

Shall they return to beatings of great bells
In wild trainloads?
A few, a few, too few for drums and yells,
May creep back, silent, to village wells
Up half-known roads.

Arms and The Boy

Wilfred Owen

Let the boy try along this bayonet-blade
How cold steel is, and keen with hunger of blood;
Blue with all malice, like a madman's flash;
And thinly drawn with famishing for flesh.

Lend him to stroke these blind, blunt bullet-heads
Which long to nuzzle in the hearts of lads,
Or give him cartridges of fine zinc teeth,
Sharp with the sharpness of grief and death.

For his teeth seem for laughing round an apple.
There lurk no claws behind his fingers supple;
And God will grow no talons at his heels,
Nor antlers through the thickness of his curls.

War Is Kind

Stephen Crane

Do not weep, maiden, for war is kind.
Because your lover threw wild hands toward the sky
And the affrighted steed ran on alone,
Do not weep.
War is kind.

> Hoarse, booming drums of the regiment,
> Little souls who thirst for fight,
> These men were born to drill and die.
> The unexplained glory flies above them,
> Great is the battle-god, great, and his kingdom–
> A field where a thousand corpses lie.

Do not weep, babe, for war is kind.
Because your father tumbled in the yellow trenches,
Raged at his breast, gulped and died,
Do not weep.
War is kind.

> Swift blazing flag of the regiment,
> Eagle with crest of red and gold,
> These men were born to drill and die.
> Point for them the virtue of slaughter,
> Make plain to them the excellence of killing
> And a field where a thousand corpses lie.

Mother whose heart hung humble as a button
On the bright splendid shroud of your son,
Do not weep.
War is kind.

Walking Wounded

Vernon Scannell

And eyes still drank the dark. They trailed the night
Along the morning road. Some limped on sticks;
Others wore rough dressings, splints and slings;
A few had turbannned heads, the dirty cloth
Brown-badged with blood. A humble brotherhood,
Not one was suffering from a lethal hurt,
They were not magnified by noble wounds,
There was no splendour in that company.
And yet, remembering after eighteen years,
In the heart's throat a sour sadness stirs;
Imagination pauses and returns
To see them walking still, but multiplied
In thousands now. And when heroic corpses
Turn slowly in their decorated sleep
And every ambulance has disappeared
The walking wounded still trudge down that lane,
And when recalled they must bear arms again.

A mammoth morning moved grey flanks and groaned.
In the rusty hedges pale rags of mist hung;
The gruel of mud and leaves in the mauled lane
Smelled sweet, like blood. Birds had died or flown,
Their green and silent attics sprouting now
With branches of leafed steel, hiding round eyes
And ripe grenades ready to drop and burst.
In the ditch at the cross-roads the fallen rider lay
Hugging his dead machine and did not stir
At crunch of mortar, tantrum of a Bren
Answering a Spandau's manic jabber.

Then into sight the ambulance came,
Stumbling and churning past the broken farm,
The amputated sign-post and smashed trees,
Slow wagonloads of bandaged cries, square trucks
That rolled on ominous wheels, vehicles
Made mythopoeic by their mortal freight
And crimson crosses on the dirty white.
This grave procession passed, though, for a while,
The grinding of their engines could be heard,
A dark noise on the pallor of the morning,
Dark as dried blood; and then it faded, died.
The road was empty, but it seemed to wait–
Like a stage which knows the cast is in the wings–
Wait for a different traffic to appear.
The mist still hung in snags from dripping thorns;
Absent-minded guns still sighed and thumped.
And then they came, the walking wounded,
Straggling the road like convicts loosely chained,
Dragging at ankles exhaustion and despair.
Their heads were weighted down by last night's lead.

Vitai Lampada

Sir Henry Newbolt

There's a breathless hush in the Close tonight–
Ten to make and the match to win–
A bumping pitch and a blinding light,
An hour to play and the last man in.
And it's not for the sake of a ribboned coat,
Or the selfish hope of a season's fame,
But his Captain's hand on his shoulder smote–
"Play up! play up! and play the game!"

The sand of the desert is sodden red,–
Red with the wreck of a square that broke;–
The Gatling's jammed and the Colonel dead,
And the regiment blind with dust and smoke.
The river of death has brimmed his banks,
And England's far and Honour a name,
But the voice of a schoolboy rallies the ranks:
"Play up! play up! and play the game!"

This is the word that year by year,
While in her place the School is set,
Every one of her sons must hear,
And none that hears it dare forget.
This they all with a joyful mind
Bear through life like a torch in flame,
And falling fling to the host behind–
"Play up! play up! and play the game!"

8

Malvina Reynolds

In Book I, we said that "New Generation" songwriters
deserve that title not only because of their age, but also
because they seek a "new generation" of life in a sterile
world. Malvina Reynolds, a California grandmother, does
not meet the first requirement for membership in this
group, but she passes the second test with bright, flying
colors. In fact, there are few songwriters whose work is
more "relevant" to what is really happening in the present
scene. Proof of the point is the selection of her songs
in this section.

Little Boxes

Words and Music by Malvina Reynolds
Malvina Reynolds Sings the Truth, Columbia CS 9414

Little boxes on the hillside,
Little boxes made of ticky tacky,
Little boxes on the hillside,
Little boxes all the same;
There's a green one and a pink one
And a blue one and a yellow one
And they're all made out of ticky tacky
And they all look just the same.

And the people in the houses
All went to the university,
Where they were put in boxes
And they came out all the same,
And there's doctors and lawyers,
And business executives,
And they're all made out of ticky tacky
And they all look just the same.

And they all play on the golf course
And drink their martinis dry,
And they all have pretty children
And the children go to school,
And the children go to summer camp
And then to the university,
Where they are put in boxes
And they come out all the same.

Little boxes on the hillside,
Little boxes made of ticky tacky,
Little boxes on the hillside,
Little boxes all the same;
And the boys go into business
And marry and raise a family
In boxes made of ticky tacky
And they all look just the same.

The Unknown Citizen

W. H. Auden

(To JS/07/M/378 This Marble Monument Is Erected by the State)
He was found by the Bureau of Statistics to be
One against whom there was no official complaint,
And all the reports on his conduct agree
That, in the modern sense of an old-fashioned word, he was a saint,
For in everything he did he served the Greater Community.
Except for the War till the day he retired
He worked in a factory and never got fired,
But satisfied his employers, Fudge Motors Inc.
Yet he wasn't a scab or odd in his views,
For his Union reports that he paid his dues,
(Our report on his Union shows it was sound)
And our Social Psychology workers found
That he was popular with his mates and liked a drink.
The Press are convinced that he bought a paper every day
And that his reactions to advertisements were normal in every way.
Policies taken out in his name prove that he was fully insured,
And his Health-card shows he was once in hospital but left it cured.
Both Producers Research and High-Grade Living declare
He was fully sensible to the advantages of the Installment Plan
And had everything necessary to the Modern Man,
A phonograph, a radio, a car and a frigidaire.
Our researchers into Public Opinion are content
That he held the proper opinions for the time of year;
When there was peace, he was for peace; when there was war, he went.
He was married and added five children to the population,
Which our Eugenist says was the right number for a parent of his generation,
And our teachers report that he never interfered with their education.
Was he free? Was he happy? The question is absurd:
Had anything been wrong, we should certainly have heard.

Sunday Morning

Seumas O'Sullivan

Outside the sunlight, outside the summer wind revelled.
Revelled and called to them, where behind dust-covered windows
They chanted
Their evening hymn.
Though it was morning,
Their thoughts were an evening hymn.
Then sudden–I heard it, I swear to you,
Sheer through the well restrained bassos–
Sheer through the delicate
Modestly mantled sopranos,
A naked voice, joyously naked,
Responsive to sunlight and summer wind suddenly thrilled.
Even so it is rumoured that once at a Sunday-school picnic
In a well-restrained gaiety nicely arranged by a river
Broke suddenly out of the forest
A naked faun.
Paused for a moment
With wonder-arched eyebrows,
Then, over the summer grass tripping
On delicate hooves,
Vanished again in the forest.

Warren Pryor

Alden Nowlan

When every pencil meant a sacrifice
his parents boarded him at school in town,
slaving to free him from the stony fields,
the meagre acreage that bore them down.

They blushed with pride when, at his graduation,
they watched him picking up the slender scroll,
his passport from the years of brutal toil
and lonely patience in a barren hole.

When he went in the Bank their cups ran over.
They marvelled how he wore a milk-white shirt
work days and jeans on Sundays. He was saved
from their thistle-strewn farm and its red dirt.

And he said nothing. Hard and serious
like a young bear inside his teller's cage,
his axe-hewn hands upon the paper bills
aching with empty strength and throttled rage.

What Have They Done to the Rain?

Words and Music by Malvina Reynolds
Malvina Reynolds Sings the Truth, Columbia CS 9414

Just a little rain
Falling on the ground,
The grass lifts its head
To the heavenly sound,
Just a little rain,
Just a little rain;
What have they done to the rain?

Just a little boy
Standing in the rain,
The gentle rain that falls for years.
And the grass is gone,
And the boy disappears,
And the rain keeps falling like helpless tears;
And what have they done to the rain?

Just a little breeze
Out of the sky,
The leaves pat their hands
As the breeze goes by,
Just a little breeze
With some smoke in its eye;
What have they done to the rain?

Just a little boy
Standing in the rain,
The gentle rain that falls for years.
And the grass is gone,
And the boy disappears,
And rain keeps falling like helpless tears;
And what have they done to the rain?

The End of the World

Archibald MacLeish

Quite unexpectedly as Vasserot
The armless ambidextrian was lighting
A match between his great and second toe
And Ralph the lion was engaged in biting
The neck of Madame Sossman while the drum
Pointed, and Teeny was about to cough
In waltz-time swinging Jocko by the thumb—
Quite unexpectedly the top blew off:

And there, there overhead, there, there, hung over
Those thousands of white faces, those dazed eyes,
There in the starless dark the poise, the hover,
There with vast wings across the canceled skies,
There in the sudden blackness the black pall
Of nothing, nothing, nothing—nothing at all.

from

Letter to the President

Walter Lowenfels

. . . What weather of shelters
        our own or anybody's analogs—
feeds down the icecaps to computers
        its song of fallout
                this spring?

What crawl of cobalt
        cracks the blood count with bells,
dissolves the crystals
        and divides the lovebirds in the laboratories
                from the dead?

Grasses that hold footprints of ants,
        neutrons where the ladybugs go,
all the jets—missiles—milk and roses
        swing an orbit of rockets
the human ear echoes when it hears
        in any isotope
or lover's touch
        the song of megatons
this spring . . .

This is the time of the limited suicide when I keep you
        from killing yourself with machine guns and bayonets,
    because I have a 100-megaton bomb produced by the Snake God
            who doesn't care how you get there–or in how many
    installments as long as the national debt passes away in
            time for another generation of shock troops to renew
                the charge.
It then becomes essential to know precisely how crazy
            the other computer is getting to be
if you want to keep the edge of deterrence open at your end.
Also, at what microsecond of the day he reaches his median,
        so you can adjust your early dew warning system to
                                    his ups and downs,
Under these circumstances, our neighbors lived a purely
                                    normal life
        the birthrate increased, the death rate declined,
        the 9% unemployment got built-in for life,
and everybody lived happily in the suburbs of forever after.

        Meanwhile
there are enough megatons in the world to kill
everybody 12 times.

        And the faintly disbelieving edges
        disappear behind the oakleaf
        where the shell on the beach bends
and the lie disappears just around the

                                    corner drug store

And the credibility of our deterrence kits

                                    will not save us

from the 11th Commandment:
        Thou Shalt Not Overkill.

Litany in Time of Plague

Thomas Nashe

Adieu, farewell earth's bliss,
This world uncertain is;
Fond are life's lustful joys,
Death proves them all but toys,
None from his darts can fly.
I am sick, I must die.
    Lord, have mercy on us!

Rich men, trust not in wealth,
Gold cannot buy you health;
Physic himself must fade,
All things to end are made.

The plague full swift goes by;
I am sick, I must die.
    Lord, have mercy on us!

Beauty is but a flower
Which wrinkles will devour:
Brightness falls from the air,
Queens have died young and fair,
Dust hath closed Helen's eye.
I am sick, I must die.
    Lord, have mercy on us!

Strength stoops unto the grave,
Worms feed on Hector brave,
Swords may not fight with fate.
Earth still holds ope her gate;
Come! come! the bells do cry.
I am sick, I must die.
    Lord, have mercy on us!

Wit with his wantonness
Tasteth death's bitterness;
Hell's executioner
Hath no ears for to hear
What vain art can reply.
I am sick, I must die.
    Lord, have mercy on us!

Haste, therefore, each degree,
To welcome destiny.
Heaven is our heritage,
Earth but a player's stage;
Mount we unto the sky.
I am sick, I must die.
    Lord, have mercy on us!

Darkness

George Gordon, Lord Byron

I had a dream, which was not all a dream.
The bright sun was extinguished, and the stars
Did wander darkling in the eternal space,
Rayless, and pathless, and the icy earth
Swung blind and blackening in the moonless air;
Morn came and went–and came, and brought no day,
And men forgot their passions in the dread
Of this their desolation; and all hearts
Were chilled into a selfish prayer for light:
And they did live by watchfires–and the thrones,
The palaces of crownéd kings–the huts,
The habitations of all things which dwell,
Were burnt for beacons; cities were consumed,
And men were gathered round their blazing homes
To look once more into each other's face;
Happy were those who dealt within the eye
Of the volcanoes, and their mountain torch:
A fearful hope was all the world contained;
Forests were set on fire–but hour by hour
They fell and faded–and the crackling trunks
Extinguished with a crash–and all was black.
The brows of men by the despairing light
Wore an unearthly aspect, as by fits
The flashes fell upon them; some lay down
And hid their eyes and wept; and some did rest
Their chins upon their clenchéd hands, and smiled;
And others hurried to and fro, and fed
Their funeral piles with fuel, and looked up
With mad disquietude on the dull sky,
The pall of a past world; and then again
With curses cast them down upon the dust,
And gnashed their teeth and howled: the wild birds shrieked
And, terrified, did flutter on the ground,
And flap their useless wings; the wildest brutes
Came tame and tremulous; and vipers crawled
And twined themselves among the multitude,
Hissing, but stingless–they were slain for food;
And War, which for a moment was no more,
Did glut himself again–a meal was bought
With blood, and each sate sullenly apart
Gorging himself in gloom: no love was left;

All earth was but one thought–and that was death
Immediate and inglorious; and the pang
Of famine fed upon all entrails–men
Died, and their bones were tombless as their flesh;
The meager by the meager were devoured,
Even dogs assailed their masters, all save one,
And he was faithful to a corse, and kept
The birds and beasts and famished men at bay,
Till hunger clung them, or the dropping dead
Lured their lank jaws; himself sought out no food,
But with a piteous and perpetual moan,
And a quick desolate cry, licking the hand
Which answered not with a caress–he died.
The crowd was famished by degrees; but two
Of an enormous city did survive,
And they were enemies: they met beside
The dying embers of an altar place,
Where had been heaped a mass of holy things
For an unholy usage; they raked up,
And shivering scraped with their cold skeleton hands
The feeble ashes, and their feeble breath
Blew for a little life, and made a flame
Which was a mockery; then they lifted up
Their eyes as it grew lighter, and beheld
Each other's aspects–saw, and shieked, and died–
Even of their mutual hideousness they died,
Unknowing who he was upon whose brow
Famine had written Fiend. The world was void,
The populous and the powerful was a lump
Seasonless, herbless, treeless, manless, lifeless–
A lump of death–a chaos of hard clay.
The rivers, lakes, and ocean all stood still,
And nothing stirred within their silent depths;
Ships sailorless lay rotting on the sea,
And their masts fell down piecemeal: as they dropped
They slept on the abyss without a surge–
The waves were dead; the tides were in their grave,
The Moon, their mistress, had expired before;
The winds were withered in the stagnant air,
And the clouds perished; Darkness had no need
Of aid from them–She was the Universe.

God Bless the Grass

Words and Music by Malvina Reynolds
Malvina Reynolds Sings the Truth, Columbia CS 9414

God bless the grass that grows through the crack,
They roll the concrete over it to try and keep it back.
The concrete gets tired of what it has to do,
It breaks and it buckles and the grass grows through,
And God bless the grass.

God bless the truth that fights toward the sun,
They roll the lies over it and think that it is done.
It moves through the ground and reaches for the air,
And after a while it is growing everywhere,
And God bless the grass.

God bless the grass that breaks through cement.
It's green and it's tender and it's easily bent,
But after a while it lifts up its head,
For the grass is living and the stone is dead,
And God bless the grass.

God bless the grass that's gentle and low,
Its roots they are deep and its will is to grow.
And God bless the truth, the friend of the poor,
And the wild grass growing at the poor man's door,
And God bless the grass.

Mater Dolorosa (Holy Saturday 1965)

Karen Lindsey

I

Around the cross
the grass is
dead.
Watered yesterday with his
blood, and your tears,
the spring-grass is brown, and
          limp   and dead.
Yesterday you wept, today you wait;
But tomorrow, Mother,
the stone will be rolled
from the tomb,
and the cruel, red wounds
transformed into radiance.
And tomorrow, the grass will live.

II

Here, in Washington,
the grass is green and
alive.
Trampled on all day by tourists,
it has risen triumphantly
after their feet have passed.
The clear, sweet odor
of the living grass
cries out to us
that we, too, are alive.

III

Mother, you wept yesterday,
and you wait today,
but tomorrow is Easter . . .

IV

On an Asian field,
the grass
is dead.
Mother, another woman
weeps, as she wept
yesterday; she waits for
nothing.
Her son is dead; in his wounds,
insects eat his flesh;
his blood and her tears
have drowned the once-green
grass
forever.
Oh, Mary,
weep for this son!
There is no angel to roll the
     stone
from his thousand tombs.

Grass

from
Song of Myself

Walt Whitman

A child said *What is the grass?* fetching it to me with full hands;
How could I answer the child? I do not know what it is any more than he.

I guess it must be the flag of my disposition, out of hopeful
    green stuff woven.
Or I guess it is the handkerchief of the Lord,
A scented gift and remembrancer designedly dropt,
Bearing the owner's name someway in the corners, that we
    may see and remark, and say *Whose?*
Or I guess the grass is itself a child, the produced babe of the vegetation.

Or I guess it is a uniform hieroglyphic,
And it means, Sprouting alike in broad zones and narrow zones,
Growing among black folks as among white,
Kanuck, Tuckahoe, Congressman, Cuff, I give them the same,
    I receive them the same.
And now it seems to me the beautiful uncut hair of graves.

Tenderly will I use you curling grass,
It may be you transpire from the breasts of young men,
It may be if I had known them I would have loved them,
It may be you are from old people, or from offspring taken
    soon out of their mothers' laps,
And here you are the mothers' laps.

This grass is very dark to be from the white heads of old mothers,
Darker than the colorless beards of old men,
Dark to come from under the faint red roofs of mouths.

O I perceive after all so many uttering tongues,
And I perceive they do not come from the roofs of mouths for nothing.
I wish I could translate the hints about the dead young men and women,
And the hints about old men and mothers, and the off-spring
    taken soon out of their laps.

What do you think has become of the young and old men?
And what do you think has become of the old women and children?

They are alive and well somewhere,
The smallest sprout shows there is really no death,
And if ever there was it led forward life, and does not wait at
   the end to arrest it,
And ceas'd the moment life appear'd.
All goes onward and outward, nothing collapses,
And to die is different from what any one supposed, and luckier.

9

Bruce MacKay

Though her population is only one-tenth that of the United States, Canada can claim a large share of the leadership for the present revolution in North American popular music. Leonard Cohen, Joni Mitchell, Buffy Sainte-Marie, Gordon Lightfoot, Ian and Sylvia, Neil Young, the Band, and the Lighthouse all have Canadian origins, and more outstanding Canadian talent is on the way.

One striking characteristic of the new Canadian songwriters is their poetic sensitivity. Bruce MacKay, Montreal film-maker and song-poet, clearly reflects this quality. Hearing the three songs reprinted in this section, the listener becomes aware of sensibility both in the social content of these songs and in the way this content is revealed. He also can discover in MacKay's songs the essential concerns and attitudes of New Generation songwriters and consequently a fair basis for judging what these young writers are trying to do.

The Half-Masted Schooner

Words and Music by Bruce MacKay
Bruce MacKay, Oro-1069 (division of ESP Records)

*When the half-masted schooner breaks upon the open shore
And your ear is half deafened by the ocean's roar
And the moon is half crazy with its own bright shine
And there's me half-twisted down the old gold mine,*

*When the dead-eyed sergeant sees his target, takes his aim
And the blind man is striking little children with his cane
And there's Jane the midnight dancer and she says you look just fine,
Ah, now, you in your small corner and I in mine,*

*And there is old Karl Marx and he is crying in his beard
And my mother is standing bravely in the storm that she has feared
And my people wrestle blindly with a kindly unseen foe,
Ah, now, if you want to follow, see my footsteps in the snow,*

*And you go to your mother, she will not understand
And you go to your father, he won't take your outstretched hand
And I shout to you sister and I say, "Don't be afraid
You're a one-man band in a two-man parade."*

*And I see you my babe, and I take you as you are
And I see you tender watching on the hill that is so far
And they are throwing stones that hurt you and the lightning flashes by,
But they'll always see you laughing and they'll never hear you cry,*

*When the missionaries come with their tongues on fire
And the morning glories grow a little higher
And the acid evangelist he talks about the Truth
To the thousand clowns who keep dancing on his roof,*

*Well now, if the lights have blinded you and you are all alone
And the hungry hands of everyone keep you from your home
And your mouth is screaming FEED ME to the flashing neon sign
You can always spend a while with me down the old gold mine.*

Prologue

Yevgeny Yevtushenko
(translated by George Reavey)

"Oh, those who are my generation!
We're not the threshold, just a step.
We're but the preface to a preface,
a prologue to a newer prologue!"

I'm many-sided.
               I'm overworked,
and idle too.
I have a goal
               and yet I'm aimless.
I don't, all of me, fit in;
               I'm awkward,
shy and rude,
nasty and goodnatured.
I love it,
            when one thing follows another
and so much of everything is mixed in me:
from West to East,
from envy to delight.
I know, you'll ask:
               "What about the integral aim?"
There's tremendous value in this all!
I'm indispensable to you!
               I'm heaped as high
as a truck with fresh mown hay!
I fly through voices,
               through branches,
                  light and chirping,
and butterflies flutter in my eyes,
                  and hay pushes out of cracks.
I greet all movement! Ardour,
and eagerness, triumphant eagerness!

Frontiers are in my way.
               It is embarrassing
for me not to know Buenos Aires and New York.
I want to walk at will
               through London,
and talk with everyone,
               even in broken English.

I want to ride
                through Paris in the morning,
hanging on to a bus like a boy.
I want art to be
                as diverse as myself;
and what if art be my torment
and harass me
                on every side,
I am already by art besieged.

I've seen myself in every aspect:
I feel kin to Yesenin
                and Walt Whitman,
to Moussorgsky grasping the whole stage,
and Gauguin's pure virgin line.

I like
        to use my skates in winter,
and, scribbling with a pen,
                                spend sleepless nights.
I like
        to defy an enemy to his face,
and bear a woman across a stream.

I bite into books, and carry firewood,
pine,
        seek something vague.

and in the August heat I love to crunch
cool scarlet slices of watermelon.

I sing and drink,
                giving no thought to death;
with arms outspread
                I fall upon the grass,
and if, this wide world, I come to die,
then I shall die from sheer joy of living.

To Althea from Prison

Richard Lovelace

When Love with unconfinèd wings
    Hovers within my gates,
And my divine Althea brings
    To whisper at the grates:
When I lie tangled in her hair,
    And fetter'd to her eye,
The birds that wanton in the air
    Know no such liberty.

When flowing cups run swiftly round
    With no allaying Thames,
Our careless heads
        with roses crowned,
    Our hearts with loyal flames;
When thirsty grief in wine we steep,
    When healths and draughts
        go free—
Fishes that tipple in the deep,
    Know no such liberty.

When, like committed linnets, I
    With shriller throat shall sing
The sweetness, mercy, majesty,
    And glories of my King;
When I shall voice aloud how good
    He is, how great should be,
Enlargèd winds that curl the flood,
    Know no such liberty.

Stone walls do not a prison make,
    Nor iron bars a cage;
Minds innocent and quiet take
    That for an hermitage;
If I have freedom in my love
    And in my soul am free,
Angels alone, that soar above,
    Enjoy such liberty.

Rubaiyat of Omar Khayyam

Edward FitzGerald
(stanzas XII-XV)

A Book of Verses underneath the Bough,
A Jug of Wine, a Loaf of Bread–and Thou
    Beside me singing in the Wilderness–
Oh, Wilderness were Paradise enow!

Some for the Glories of This World; and some
Sigh for the Prophet's Paradise to come;
    Ah, take the Cash, and let the Credit go,
Nor heed the rumble of a distant Drum!

Look to the blowing Rose about us–"Lo,
Laughing," she says, "into the world I blow,
    At once the silken tassel of my Purse
Tear, and its Treasure on the Garden throw."

And those who husbanded the Golden grain,
And those who flung it to the winds like Rain,
    Alike to no such aureate Earth are turned
As, buried once, Men want dug up again.

The Sacraments of Evil

Words and Music by Bruce MacKay
Bruce MacKay Is, Gamma GS 501

Now the worldly powers talk in their towers,
But tell me what is said,
And when they see it's too late to forget their hate
Their words will all be dead.
And the park bench rub, he's got no tub
Where he can wash himself,
Now he's out of touch and he don't say much,
But the language of rags can speak for itself.

> *But what can you say,*
> *My little high hat queen?*
> *But what can you say*
> *After seeing all you've seen?*
> *And you do not want to answer,*
> *I don't think you ever will,*
> *And you don't even cry*
> *When you're surrounded by*
> *The sacraments of evil.*

Now a southern wind has colored the skin
Of people just like you,
So you've taken your guns and you've shot at the ones
Who won't do what you want them to.
And when the defendant's tried for homicide
The jury's his clan and the judge is his pa
And when he's set free, don't ask me
What I call your law.

But what can you say,
My little high hat queen?
But what can you say
After seeing all you've seen?
And you do not want to answer
Are you afraid of your good people?
And in the silence of night,
You're helping to write
The sacraments of evil.

Now a million men are dead 'cause when
They're told to fight they're afraid to talk,
And in religious bliss, death has kissed
Them hard and cold as rock,
And the bread is broken with no word spoken
In a silent communion song,
But what hurts most is that we are the host
From whom the blood is drawn.

But what can you say,
My little high hat queen?
But what can you say
After seeing all you've seen?
And do you do want to answer,
Are you afraid your blood will be spilled
By the Lord High Priest
Who watches over the feast
In the sacraments of evil?

The Landscape near an Aerodrome

Stephen Spender

More beautiful and soft than any moth
With burning furred antennae feeling its huge path
Through dusk, the air liner with shut-off engines
Glides over suburbs and the sleeves set trailing tall
To point the wind. Gently, broadly, she falls,
Scarcely disturbing charted currents of air.

Lulled by descent, the travellers across sea
And across feminine land indulging its easy limbs
In miles of softness, now let their eyes trained by watching
Penetrate through dusk the outskirts of this town
Here where industry shows a fraying edge.
Here they may see what is being done.

Beyond the winking masthead light
And the landing ground, they observe the outposts
Of work: chimneys like lank black fingers
Or figures, frightening and mad: and squat buildings
With their strange air behind trees, like women's faces
Shattered by grief. Here where few houses
Moan with faint light behind their blinds,
They remark the unhomely sense of complaint, like a dog
Shut out, and shivering at the foreign moon.

In the last sweep of love, they pass over fields
Behind the aerodrome, where boys play all day
Hacking dead grass: whose cries, like wild birds,
Settle upon the nearest roofs
But soon are hid under the loud city.

Then, as they land, they hear the tolling bell
Reaching across the landscape of hysteria,
To where, louder than all those batteries
And charcoaled towers against that dying sky,
Religion stands, the Church blocking the sun.

The Snow Man

Wallace Stevens

One must have a mind of winter
To regard the frost and the boughs
Of the pine-trees crusted with snow;

And have been cold a long time
To behold the junipers shagged with ice,
The spruces rough in the distant glitter

Of the January sun; and not to think
Of any misery in the sound of the wind,
In the sound of a few leaves,

Which is the sound of the land
Full of the same wind
That is blowing in the same bare place

For the listener, who listens in the snow,
And, nothing himself, beholds
Nothing that is not there and the nothing that is.

Living for Others

Laotse
(Translated by Lin Yutang)

The universe is everlasting.
The reason the universe is everlasting
    Is that it does not live for Self.
Therefore it can long endure.

Therefore the Sage puts himself last,
    And finds himself in the foremost place;
Regards his body as accidental,
    And his body is thereby preserved.
Is it not because he does not live for Self
That his Self is realized.

Song of the Black Veils

Words and Music by Bruce MacKay
Bruce MacKay Is, Gamma GS 501

Take your black veils
And take your black gloves
And start to put them on,
Cry for your husbands
And cry for your sons
And cry for the ones who won't be coming home.

Bring back the wounded
And bury your dead,
Wash away the blood and the pain,
Say once more
What you've always said,
That you'll never let them fight again.

Forget that you've mourned,
Oh forget all your tears,
Forget that you've cried and you've prayed,
Take off your veils,
And take off your gloves,
And dance around the funeral pyre you've made.

Notes for a Movie Script

M. Carl Holman

Fade in the sound of summer music,
Picture a hand plunging through her hair,
Next his socked feet and her scuffed dance slippers
Close, as they kiss on the rug-stripped stair.

Catch now the taxi from the station,
Capture her shoulders' sudden sag;
Switch to him silent in the barracks
While the room roars at the corporal's gag.

Let the drums dwindle in the distance,
Pile the green sea above the land;
While she prepares a single breakfast,
Reading the V mail in her hand.

Ride a cold moonbeam to the pillbox,
Sidle the camera to his feet
Sprawled just outside in the gummy grasses,
Swollen like nightmare and not neat.

Now doorbell nudges the lazy morning:
She stills the sweeper for a while,
Twitches her dress, swings the screendoor open,
Cut--with no music--on her smile.

For the Fallen

Laurence Binyon

With proud thanksgiving, a mother for her children,
England mourns for her dead across the sea.
Flesh of her flesh they were, spirit of her spirit,
Fallen in the cause of the free.

Solemn the drums thrill: Death august and royal
Sings sorrow up into immortal spheres.
There is music in the midst of desolation
And a glory that shines upon our tears.

They went with songs to the battle, they were young,
Straight of limb, true of eye, steady and aglow
They were staunch to the end against odds uncounted,
They fell with their faces to the foe.

They shall not grow old, as we that are left grow old:
Age shall not weary them, nor the years condemn.
At the going down of the sun and in the morning
We will remember them.

They mingle not with their laughing comrades again;
They sit no more at familiar tables at home;
They have no lot in our labour of the day-time;
They sleep beyond England's foam.

But where our desires are and our hopes profound,
Felt as a well-spring that is hidden from sight,
To the innermost heart of their own land they are known
As the stars are known to the Night;

As the stars that shall be bright when we are dust,
Moving in marches upon the starry plain,
As the stars that are starry in the time of our darkness,
To the end, to the end, they remain.

To Lucasta, On Going to the Wars

Richard Lovelace

Tell me not, sweet, I am unkind,
   That from the nunnery
Of thy chaste breast and quiet mind
   To war and arms I fly.

True, a new mistress now I chase,
   The first foe in the field;
And with a stronger faith embrace
   A sword, a horse, a shield.

Yet this inconstancy is such
   As thou too shalt adore:
I could not love thee, dear, so much,
   Loved I not honour more.

To the Glorious Dead

Judi Vyse

The Glorious Dead
Are a useful lot–
The ones who were lost
On the place they fought.

They give us a place
In the crowded downtown
To set our pansies
That wilt when they've grown.

They give us a stone
With steps up the front
A place to pose
With "Fortissimi Sunt".

In a red-light pause
Around the step
Pansies planted–
"Lest We Forget".

What Were They Like?
(Questions and Answers)

Denise Levertov

1) Did the people of Viet Nam
   use lanterns of stone?
2) Did they hold ceremonies
   to reverence the opening of buds?
3) Were they inclined to rippling laughter?
4) Did they use bone and ivory,
   jade and silver, for ornament?
5) Had they an epic poem?
6) Did they distinguish between speech and singing?

1) Sir, their light hearts turned to stone.
   It is not remembered whether in gardens
   stone lanterns illumined pleasant ways.
2) Perhaps they gathered once to delight in blossom,
   But after the children were killed
   there were no more buds.
3) Sir, laughter is bitter to the burned mouth.
4) A dream ago, perhaps. Ornament is for joy.
   All the bones were charred.
5) It is not remembered. Remember,
   most were peasants; their life
   was in rice and bamboo.
   When peaceful clouds were reflected in the paddies
   and the water-buffalo stepped surely along terraces,
   maybe fathers told their sons old tales.
   When bombs smashed the mirrors
   there was time only to scream.
6) There is an echo yet, it is said,
   of their speech which was like a song.
   It is reported their singing resembled
   the flight of moths in moonlight.
   Who can say? It is silent now.

10

David Crosby

New Generation songwriters are keenly aware of how risky
it is to open one's heart to others in a society where people
are constantly taking psychic advantages of one another.
At the same time, they are acutely sensitive to the dangers
of cutting one's self off from society. David Crosby's
Mind Gardens is a song reflecting the tensions between
these two awarenesses. Notice how differently the theme
of isolation is treated in the older poems accompanying
this song.

Crosby, formerly with *The Byrds,* is now a member of the
"supergroup", *Crosby, Stills, Nash, and Young.*

Mind Gardens

Words and Music by David Crosby
The Byrds, *Younger than Yesterday*, Columbia CS 9442

Once upon a time there was a garden
On a high hill green and bluff and round against the sea
There the sun came and the rain pourin' down
Garden grew and flourished and splattered bits of color on the ground
And it took shape in symmetry and all of life abound
But there came winds driven and howling there came snow
And I feared for the garden so I built a wall
Kept it from the slings and arrows of outrageous fortune
The killin' cold could not get in
But when the sun came and the gentle rain of spring
They could not reach the garden behind those walls
It would have died safely securely died
But as I watched and as I learned
I tore the walls all down
The garden still lives

The Road

James Stephens

Because our lives are cowardly and sly,
Because we do not dare to take or give,
Because we scowl and pass each other by,
We do not live; we do not dare to live.

We dive, each man, into his secret house,
And bolt the door, and listen in affright,
Each timid man beside a timid spouse,
With timid children huddled out of sight.

Kissing in secret, fighting secretly!
We crawl and hide like vermin in a hole,
Under the bravery of sun and sky,
We flash our meannesses of face and soul.

Let us go out and walk upon the road,
And quit for evermore the brick-built den,
And lock and key, the hidden, shy abode
That separates us from our fellow-men.

And by contagion of the sun we may,
Catch at a spark from that primeval fire,
And learn that we are better than our clay,
And equal to the peaks of our desire.

The Garden of Love

William Blake

I went to the Garden of Love,
And saw what I never had seen:
A Chapel was built in the midst,
Where I used to play on the green.

And the gates of this Chapel were shut,
And Thou shalt not, writ over the door;
So I turn'd to the Garden of Love,
That so many sweet flowers bore,

And I saw it was filled with graves,
And tomb-stones where flowers should be:
And Priests in black gowns, were walking their rounds,
And binding with briars, my joys & desires.

Truth

Uta Peikert

The wind blows,
In December,
Holding the truth,
For you to feel;
And if your shelter walls
Are thick–
Forget the truth;
It's lost to you.

Ode on Solitude

Alexander Pope

Happy the man, whose wish and care
    A few paternal acres bound,
Content to breathe his native air,
        In his own ground.

Whose herds with milk, whose fields with bread,
    Whose flocks supply him with attire,
Whose trees in summer yield him shade,
        In winter fire.

Blest, who can unconcern'dly find,
    Hours, days and years slide soft away,
In health of body, peace of mind,
        Quiet by day,

Sound sleep by night; study and ease,
    Together mixt; sweet recreation;
And innocence which most does please,
        With meditation.

Thus let me live, unseen, unknown,
    Thus unlamented let me die,
Steal from the world, and not a stone
        Tell where I lie.

11

Stephen Stills

Recognized first for his work with the now disbanded *Buffalo Springfield,* Stephen Stills is today becoming known as one of the leading New Generation songwriters. *For What It's Worth,* now a rock classic, was written by Stills as a reaction to the first major demonstrations that took place on the Berkeley campus of the University of California. Called to support freedom of speech on that campus, these demonstrations triggered the "student power" movement. *For What It's Worth,* however, is not just a topical song. Its principal object is social paranoia, perhaps the most dangerous disease of our time. Furthermore, the significant insights of the song find a pecuiarly "right" sort of expression in Stills' rock-style rhythms and lyrics—which suggests perhaps that rock itself has a paranoid potential.

For What It's Worth

Words and Music by Stephen Stills
The Buffalo Springfield, *Buffalo Springfield*, Atco SD 33-200

There's something happening here,
There's a man with a gun over there
Tellin' me I've got to beware.

I think it's time we—
Stop children, what's that sound?
Ev'rybody look what's goin' down.

There's battle lines bein' drawn,
Nobody's right if ev'rybody's wrong,
Young people speakin' their minds,
Gettin' so much resistance from behind.

I think it's time we—
Stop children, what's that sound?
Ev'rybody look what's goin' down.

What a field day for the heat!
A thousand people in the street
Singin' songs and carryin' signs,
Mostly saying, "Hooray for our side."

I think it's time we—
Stop children, what's that sound?
Ev'rybody look what's goin' down.

Paranoia strikes deep,
Into your life it will creep,
It starts when you're always afraid,
Step out of line the men come and take you away.

You better—
Stop! Hey, what's that sound?
Ev'rybody look what's goin' down.

Diary of a Nerve

Kenneth McRobbie

Monday's run on biographies significant.
Caught a librarian crying.
                  It was not
Clear why the old men seized the Reference Room.
Too-long cigarette ends in too-full plates.
Mother acting strange. Mustn't
                    sleep in so late.

Tuesday proves the library is affected.
Breathing from *that* room.
                  So I fled
When operators sang in the mortal exchanges,
And something moved in the catalogue.
Current failing in the suburbs,
                  the wires sob.

Wednesday, Wednesday, I'll always remember
Youths in their crawl stroke surging
                  once the girls' wonder
Now drafted into requisitioned rooming houses,
Their wood-green pool forgotten at high tide
As they add and write, the nervous
                  sea's skin beside.

Advertisers move out, silencing Thursday.
The smudged news worries
                  caretakers by
Stair lights burning in the glass stories.
Paint flakes from all late model cars.
Exhausts obliterate
                  sidewalks, stars.

Should have heard of this before Friday
               in order to–
How bones were found gnawed by the campfire,
Weapons within reach.
                  No one can get through now.
The cat has broken all its legs.
I'm alone in a room.
               Who will read this?

It's today. All cover the beaches with no word.
The freighter from horizon heaving
               enters the fiord.
The quay falls to a strange cheering.
A bell rings once in the deserted
               downstairs–and no more,
As I turn at last
               to look at my stirring door.

September, 1802

William Wordsworth

O Friend! I know not which way I must look
    For comfort, being, as I am, opprest,
    To think that now our life is only drest
For show; mean handy-work of craftsman, cook,
Or groom!–We must run glittering like a brook
    In the open sunshine, or we are unblest:
    The wealthiest man among us is the best:
No grandeur now in nature or in book
Delights us. Rapine, avarice, expense,
    This is idolatry; and these we adore.
    Plain living and high thinking are no more:
The homely beauty of the good old cause
Is gone; our peace, our fearful innocence,
    And pure religion breathing household laws.

A Ritual To Read to Each Other

William Stafford

If you don't know the kind of person I am
and I don't know the kind of person you are
a pattern that others made may prevail in the world
and following the wrong god home we may miss our star.

For there is many a small betrayal in the mind,
a shrug that lets the fragile sequence break
sending with shouts the horrible errors of childhood
storming out to play through the broken dyke.

And as elephants parade holding each elephant's tail,
but if one wanders the circus won't find the park,
I call it cruel and maybe the root of all cruelty
to know what occurs but not recognize the fact.

And so I appeal to a voice, to something shadowy,
a remote important region in all who talk:
though we could fool each other, we should consider–
lest the parade of our mutual life get lost in the dark.

For it is important that awake people be awake,
or a breaking line may discourage them back to sleep;
the signals we give–yes or no, or maybe–
should be clear: the darkness around us is deep.

from
Windsor Forest

Alexander Pope

The time shall come, when free as seas or wind
unbounded Thames shall flow for all mankind,
Whole nations enter with each swelling tide,
And seas but join the regions they divide;
Earth's distant ends our glory shall behold,
And the new world launch forth to seek the old.
Then ships of uncouth form shall stem the tide,
And feather'd people crowd my wealthy side,
And naked youths and painted chiefs admire
Our speech, our colour, and our strange attire!
Oh stretch thy reign, fair Peace! from shore to shore,
'Till Conquest cease, and Slav'ry be no more;
'Till the freed Indians in their native groves
Reap their own fruits, and woo their sable loves,
Peru once more a race of Kings behold,
And other Mexico's be roof'd with gold.
Exil'd by thee from earth to deepest hell,
In brazen bonds, shall barb'rous Discord dwell;
Gigantic Pride, pale Terror, gloomy Care,
And mad Ambition shall attend her there:
There purple Vengeance bath'd in gore retires,
Her weapons blunted, and extinct her fires:
There hateful Envy her own snakes shall feel,
And Persecution mourn her broken wheel:
There Faction roar, Rebellion bite her chain,
And gasping Furies thirst for blood in vain.

A Kingdom for Mr. Bojangles

for Martin

Penelope Schafer

The world is too much with us
a violence erupts; to change or burn
He dances free on the stage of apathy
while anarchy rides the concrete jungle
and the pre-war assembly gathers.
The children of hope are infected with power
drenched in the ritual of mind
trading worn out toys for verbal noise.

The cancer is spreading;
frustrated cops are seeking the doctor,
the black man is homeless
waiting to be born again
outside the kingdom of agony.

A man wreathed in the gravestones of love
who knew sacrifice and God,
saw the light beckon
in a harmless humanity.
He has gone from us all
yet circles us like a pitfall.

We are like dying children
being smothered alive
who forget what it means to be free.
Listen to the sounds of willed vibrations,
mournful sinners
sing in praise
hold flowers and learn to walk.
We will weave stitches of struggle
and ask how the many
can become the One?

12

Paul Simon

The work of the immensely popular singer-composer
Paul Simon is represented here by the song, *Old Friends,*
lyrically one of the best selections from the finest Simon
and Garfunkel album to date, *Bookends.* In order to
appreciate the full impact of that song, it is essential that
one first hear the cut that precedes it, *Voices of Old
People.* These are the sounds of the reality that Simon
contemplates in his song, a reality that is probably too
remote from the experiences of youth to be conveyed by
the usual devices of art. Having listened, however, to the
actual voices of the aged, a young person gains clear
intimations of mortality, which Simon's song can then
meaningfully develop for him. The poems accompanying
Old Friends make it possible to travel still farther across
the bridges of time.

Old Friends

Words and Music by Paul Simon
Simon and Garfunkel, *Bookends*, Columbia KCS 9529

Old friends,
Old friends,
Sat on their park bench
Like bookends.
A newspaper blown through the grass
Falls on the round toes
Of the high shoes
Of the old friends.

Old friends,
Winter companions,
The old men
Lost in their overcoats,
Waiting for the sunset.
The sounds of the city,
Sifting through trees,
Settle like dust
On the shoulders
Of the old friends.

Can you imagine us
Years from today,
Sharing a park bench quietly?
How terribly strange
To be seventy.

Old friends,
Memory brushes the same years.
Silently sharing the same fear. . . .

Mr Flood's Party

Edwin Arlington Robinson

Old Eben Flood, climbing alone one night
Over the hill between the town below
And the forsaken upland hermitage
That held as much as he should ever know
On earth again of home, paused warily.
The road was his with not a native near;
And Eben, having leisure, said aloud,
For no man else in Tilbury Town to hear:

"Well, Mr Flood, we have the harvest moon
Again, and we may not have many more;
The bird is on the wing, the poet says,
And you and I have said it here before.
Drink to the bird." He raised up to the light
The jug that he had gone so far to fill,
And answered huskily: "Well, Mr Flood,
Since you propose it, I believe I will."

Alone, as if enduring to the end
A valiant armour of scarred hopes outworn,
He stood there in the middle of the road
Like Roland's ghost winding a silent horn.
Below him, in the town among the trees,
Where friends of other days had honored him,
A phantom salutation of the dead
Rang thinly till old Eben's eyes were dim.

Then, as a mother lays her sleeping child
Down tenderly, fearing it may awake,
He set the jug down slowly at his feet
With trembling care, knowing that most things break;
And only when assured that on firm earth
It stood, as the uncertain lives of men
Assuredly did not, he paced away,
And with his hand extended paused again:

"Well, Mr Flood, we have not met like this
In a long time; and many a change has come
To both of us, I fear, since last it was
We had a drop together. Welcome home!"
Convivially returning with himself,
Again he raised the jug up to the light;
And with an acquiescent quaver said:
"Well, Mr Flood, if you insist, I might."

"Only a very little, Mr Flood—
For auld lang syne. No more, sir; that will do."
So, for the time, apparently it did,
And Eben evidently thought so too;
For soon amid the silver loneliness
Of night he lifted up his voice and sang,
Secure, with only two moons listening,
Until the whole harmonious landscape rang—

'For auld lang syne.' The weary throat gave out,
The last word wavered, and the song was done.
He raised again the jug regretfully
And shook his head, and was again alone.
There was not much that was ahead of him,
And there was nothing in the town below—
Where strangers would have shut the many doors
That many friends had opened long ago.

When I See Old Men

Raymond Souster

When I see old men
with noses in books
every night in dead corners
of deserted rooms;

when I watch the look
they give the young girls
passing in the street
that end in sigh;

when I hear the petty boasting
a glass of beer lights in them,
the inevitable memories
of their once greatness;

then I pray that my old age
shall be brief as the fluke
matador's one golden season,
the year unmarked by horns
overflowing with contracts
and cries that echo
round the hoarse arena.

from

The Garden of Proserpine

Algernon Charles Swinburne

We are not sure of sorrow,
    And joy was never sure;
To-day will die to-morrow;
    Time stoops to no man's lure;
And love, grown faint and fretful,
With lips but half regretful
Sighs, and with eyes forgetful
    Weeps that no loves endure.

From too much love or living,
    From hope and fear set free,
We thank with brief thanksgiving
    Whatever gods may be
That no life lives for ever;
That dead men rise up never;
That even the weariest river
    Winds somewhere safe to sea.

Then star nor sun shall waken,
    Nor any change of light:
Nor sound of waters shaken,
    Nor any sound or sight:
Nor wintry leaves nor vernal,
Nor days nor things diurnal;
Only the sleep eternal
    In an eternal night.

Promise of Peace

Robinson Jeffers

The heads of strong old age are beautiful
Beyond all grace of youth. They have strange quiet,
Integrity, health, soundness, to the full
They've dealt with life and been attempered by it.
A young man must not sleep; his years are war
Civil and foreign but the former's worse;
But the old can breathe in safety now that they are
Forgetting what youth meant, the being perverse,
Running the fool's gauntlet and being cut
By the whips of the five senses. As for me,
If I should wish to live long it were but
To trade those fevers for tranquility,
Thinking though that's entire and sweet in the grave
How shall the dead taste the deep treasure they have?

I Heard a Fly Buzz When I Died

Emily Dickenson

I heard a fly buzz when I died;
The stillness in the room
Was like the stillness in the air
Between the heaves of storm.

The eyes around had wrung them dry,
And breaths were gathering firm
For that last onset, when the king
Be witnessed in the room.

I willed my keepsakes, signed away
What portion of me be
Assignable–and then it was
There interposed a fly,

With blue, uncertain, stumbling buzz,
Between the light and me;
And then the windows failed, and then
I could not see to see.

13

Mick Jagger

We said that the first group of songwriters in this book expressed what the early Christians called "agape" —concern for the family of man. Another Greek word might identify our next theme. In this and the following chapters, Mick Jagger, the *Cream,* Harry Nilsson, Bob Lind, and Leonard Cohen explore "eros"—the principle of sexual and aesthetic love.

Famed for their raw, driving power, the *Rolling Stones* have frequently been said to lead the primitives of English rock, in contrast to the *Beatles,* who set the pace for the sophisticated. The fact is, however, that the *Rolling Stones'* lyricist, Mick Jagger, has written some of the subtlest love songs of the last decade. Here we present three of the best known: *Lady Jane, Paint It Black,* and *Ruby Tuesday.*

Lady Jane exploits a distinction in poetic form that, though always present, rarely becomes an issue for poetic experience, namely, the distinction between author and dramatic speaker. The latter is the character who *appears* to be expressing himself; the former is the person who actually created the poem. Technically, a difference is always possible between what they are attempting to do; in the typical popular song, for example, the "I" in the lyric is generally trying to justify himself, whereas the real author is hoping that we find the "I" to be an appealing character. Normally, the difference does not much matter to the audience. In *Lady Jane,* however, the difference is crucial. The attempt of Jagger's dramatic speaker to justify himself is in fact the very means by which Jagger condemns him, and so we must continually interpret what the speaker says in terms of how Jagger is criticizing the typical aristocratic cad whom the speaker represents.

Paint It Black performs one of the most important functions of poetry—the revivification of old metaphors, customs, and traditions. Black, of course, is the color of mourning, but the fact that we can say "of course" shows that the rightness of this association between black and mourning has probably been obscured for us by long familiarity. Jagger makes us rediscover that rightness. Using hard rock rhythms to beat out rage and grief, Jagger shows how naturally these emotions turn against light when light denies itself to someone we loved.

Ruby Tuesday attracts us because of not only the girl's interesting character but also the attitude the poet takes to her. In conventional popular songs freedom-loving women like Ruby Tuesday are regarded as butterflies, *femmes fatales,* teasers, or, more kindly, girls who have yet to find the "right" man. Jagger, however, treats this kind of person with genuine respect. He lets her *be.* At the same time, his admiration for her is touched with desire so that there is a certain poignant character to his feeling. The undeniable health and freshness of this attitude wins our approval—and perhaps even makes us a little ashamed if we are possessive in our relationships.

Paint It Black

Words and Music by Mick Jagger and Keith Richards
The Rolling Stones, *Aftermath*, London 476

I see a red door and I want it painted black,
No colors any more, I want them to turn black.
I see the girls walk by dressed in their summer clothes.
I have to turn my head until my darkness goes.

I see a line of cars and they're all painted black,
With flowers and my love both never to come back.
I see people turn their heads and quickly look away,
Like a new born baby it just happens ev'ry day.

I look inside myself and see my heart is black,
I see my red door and I want it painted black.
Maybe then I'll fade away and not have to face the facts,
It's not easy facing up when your whole world is black.

No more will my green sea go turn a deeper blue,
I could not foresee this thing happening to you.
If I look hard enough into the setting sun,
My love will laugh with me before the morning comes.

I see a red door and I want it painted black,
No colors any more, I want them to turn black.
I see the girls walk by dressed in their summer clothes,
I have to turn my head until the darkness goes.
I wanna see your face painted black, black as night.
Don't wanna see the sun flyin' high in the sky,
I wanna see it painted, painted, painted, painted black!

Grief, Find the Words

Sir Philip Sidney

Grief, find the words; for thou hast made my brain
So dark with misty vapors which arise
From out thy heavy mould, that inbent eyes
Can scarce discern the shape of mine own pain.
Do thou, then–for thou canst–do thou complain
For my poor soul, which now that sickness tries
Which even to sense, sense of itself denies,
Though harbingers of death lodge there his train.
Or if thy love of plaint yet mine forbears,
As of a caitiff worthy so to die,
Yet wail thyself, and wail with causeful tears,
That though in wretchedness thy life doth lie
Yet grow'st more wretched than thy nature bears
By being placed in such a wretch as I.

A Slumber Did My Spirit Seal

William Wordsworth

A slumber did my spirit seal;
    I had no human fears:
She seemed a thing that could not feel
    The touch of earthly years.

No motion has she now, no force;
    She neither hears nor sees;
Rolled round in earth's diurnal course,
    With rocks, and stones, and trees.

from

In Memoriam

Alfred, Lord Tennyson

(VII, LIV-LVI)

Dark house, by which once more I stand
   Here in the long unlovely street,
   Doors, where my heart was used to beat
So quickly, waiting for a hand,

A hand that can be clasped no more–
   Behold me, for I cannot sleep,
   And like a guilty thing I creep
At earliest morning to the door.

He is not here; but far away
   The noise of life begins again,
   And ghastly through the drizzling rain
On the bald street breaks the blank day.

        • • •

O, yet we trust that somehow good
   Will be the final goal of ill,
   To pangs of nature, sins of will,
Defects of doubt, and taints of blood;

That nothing walks with aimless feet;
   That not one life shall be destroyed,
   Or cast as rubbish to the void,
When God hath made the pile complete;

That not a worm is cloven in vain;
   That not a moth with vain desire
   Is shrivelled in a fruitless fire,
Or but subserves another's gain.

Behold, we know not anything;
   I can but trust that good shall fall
   At last–far off–at last, to all.
And every winter change to spring.

So runs my dream; but what am I?
   An infant crying in the night;
   An infant crying for the light,
And with no language but a cry.

The wish, that of the living whole
  No life may fail beyond the grave,
  Derives it not from what we have
The likest God within the soul?

Are God and Nature then at strife,
  That Nature lends such evil dreams?
  So careful of the type she seems,
So careless of the single life,

That I, considering everywhere
  Her secret meaning in her deeds,
  And finding that of fifty seeds
She often brings but one to bear,

I falter where I firmly trod,
  And falling with my weight of cares
  Upon the great world's altar-stairs
That slope through darkness up to God,

I stretch lame hands of faith, and grope,
  And gather dust and chaff, and call
  To what I feel is Lord of all,
And faintly trust the larger hope.

"So careful of the type?" but no,
  From scarped cliff and quarried stone
  She cries, "A thousand types are gone:
I care for nothing, all shall go.

"Thou makest thine appeal to me:
  I bring to life, I bring to death:
  The spirit does but mean the breath
I know no more." And he, shall be,

Man, her last work, who seemed so fair,
  Such splendid purpose in his eyes,
  Who rolled the psalm to wintry skies,
Who built him fanes of fruitless prayer,

Who trusted God was love indeed
  And love Creation's final law–
  Though Nature, red in tooth and claw
With ravine, shrieked against his creed–

Who loved, who suffered countless ills,
  Who battled for the True, the Just,
  Be blown about the desert dust,
Or sealed within the iron hills?

No more? A monster then, a dream,
  A discord. Dragons of the prime,
  That tare each other in their slime,
Were mellow music match'd with him.

O life as futile, then, as frail!
  O for thy voice to soothe and bless!
  What hope of answer, or redress?
Behind the veil, behind the veil.

Methought I Saw My Late Espoused Saint

John Milton

Methought I saw my late espousèd saint
   Brought to me like Alcestis from the grave,
   Whom Jove's great son to her glad husband gave,
   Rescued from death by force though pale and faint.
Mine, as whom washed from spot of childbed taint,
   Purification in the old law did save,
   And such, as yet once more I trust to have
   Full sight of her in Heaven without restraint,
Came vested all in white, pure as her mind.
   Her face was veiled, yet to my fancied sight,
   Love, sweetness, goodness, in her person shined
So clear, as in no face with more delight.
   But O, as to embrace me she inclined,
   I waked, she fled, and day brought back my night.

Sic Vita

Henry King

Like to the falling of a star,
Or as the flights of eagles are,
Or like the fresh spring's gaudy hue,
Or silver drops of morning dew,
Or like a wind that chafes the flood,
Or bubbles which on water stood:
Even such is man, whose borrowed light
Is straight called in, and paid to night.
   The wind blows out, the bubble dies;
   The spring entombed in autumn lies;
   The dew dries up, the star is shot;
   The flight is past, and man forgot.

Ruby Tuesday

Words and Music by Mick Jagger
The Rolling Stones, *Between the Buttons,* London 499

She would never say where she came from,
Yesterday don't matter if it's gone,
While the sun is bright or in the darkest night
No one knows, she comes and goes.

> *Chorus:*
>
> *Goodbye, Ruby Tuesday,*
> *Who could hang a name on you*
> *When you change with every new day?*
> *Still, I am going to miss you.*

Don't question why she needs to be so free,
She'll tell you it's the only way to be,
She just can't be chained to a life where nothing is gained
And nothing is lost at such a cost.

> *Chorus*

There's no time to lose, I heard her say,
Cash your dreams before they slip away,
Dying all the time, lose your dreams and you will lose your mind—
Ain't life unkind?

> *Chorus*

On the Move

'Man, you gotta Go.'

Thom Gunn

The blue jay scuffling in the bushes follows
Some hidden purpose, and the gust of birds
That spurts across the field, the wheeling swallows,
Have nested in the trees and undergrowth.
Seeking their instinct, or their poise, or both,
One moves with an uncertain violence
Under the dust thrown by a baffled sense
Or the dull thunder of approximate words.

On motorcycles, up the road, they come:
Small, black, as flies hanging in heat, the Boys,
Until the distance throws them forth, their hum
Bulges to thunder held by calf and thigh.
In goggles, donned impersonality,
In gleaming jackets trophied with the dust,
They strap in doubt–by hiding it, robust–
And almost hear a meaning in their noise.

Exact conclusion of their hardiness
Has no shape yet, but from known whereabouts
They ride, direction where the tyres press.
They scare a flight of birds across the field:
Much that is natural, to the will must yield.
Men manufacture both machine and soul,
And use what they imperfectly control
To dare a future from the taken routes.

It is a part solution, after all.
One is not necessarily discord
On earth; or damned because, half animal
One lacks direct instinct, because one wakes
Afloat on movement that divides and breaks.
One joins the movement in a valueless world,
Choosing it, till, both hurler and the hurled,
One moves as well, always toward, toward.

A minute holds them, who have come to go:
The self-defined, astride the created will
They burst away; the towns they travel through
Are home for neither bird nor holiness,
For birds and saints complete their purposes.
At worst, one is in motion; and at best,
Reaching no absolute, in which to rest,
One is always nearer by not keeping still.

My Mind to Me a Kingdom Is

Sir Edward Dyer

My mind to me a kingdom is;
    Such present joys therein I find
That it excels all other bliss
    That earth affords or grows by kind:
Though much I want which most would have,
Yet still my mind forbids to crave.

No princely pomp, no wealthy store,
    No force to win the victory,
No wily wit to salve a sore,
    No shape to feed a loving eye;
To none of these I yield as thrall:
For why? My mind doth serve for all.

I see how plenty suffers oft,
    And hasty climbers soon do fall;
I see that those which are aloft
    Mishap doth threaten most of all;
They get with toil, they keep with fear:
Such cares my mind could never bear.

Content I live, this is my stay;
    I seek no more than may suffice;
I press to bear no haughty sway;
    Look, what I lack my mind supplies:
Lo, thus I triumph like a king,
Content with that my mind doth bring.

Some have too much, yet still do crave;
   I little have, and seek no more.
They are but poor, though much they have,
   And I am rich with little store:
They poor, I rich; they beg, I give;
They lack, I leave; they pine, I live.

I laugh not at another's loss;
   I grudge not at another's gain;
No worldly waves my mind can toss;
   My state at one doth still remain:
I fear no foe, I fawn no friend;
I loathe not life, nor dread my end.

Some weigh their pleasure by their lust,
   Their wisdom by their rage of will;
Their treasure is their only trust;
   A cloakèd craft their store of skill:
But all the pleasure that I find
Is to maintain a quiet mind.

My wealth is health and perfect ease;
   My conscience clear my choice defence;
I neither seek by bribes to please,
   Nor by deceit to breed offence:
Thus do I live; thus will I die;
Would all did so as well as I!

Farewell! Thou Art Too Dear for My Possessing

William Shakespeare

Farewell! Thou art too dear for my possessing,
And like enough thou know'st thy estimate.
The charter of thy worth gives thee releasing,
My bonds in thee are all determinate.
For how do I hold thee but by thy granting?
And for that riches where is my deserving?
The cause of this fair gift in me is wanting,
And so my patent back again is swerving.
Thyself thou gavest, thy own worth then not knowing,
Or me, to whom thou gavest it, else mistaking.
So thy great gift, upon misprision growing,
Comes home again, on better judgment making.
   Thus have I had thee, as a dream doth flatter,
   In sleep a king, but waking no such matter.

Lady Jane

Words and Music by Mick Jagger
The Rolling Stones, *Aftermath*, London 476

My sweet Lady Jane, when I see you again,
Your servant am I and will humbly remain,
Just heed this plea my love,
On bended knee my love,
I pledge my troth to Lady Jane.

My dear Lady Ann, I've done what I can,
I must take my leave for promised I am,
This play is run my love,
Your time has come my love,
I've pledged my troth to Lady Jane.

Oh my sweet Marie, I wait at your ease,
The sands have run out for your lady and me,
Wedlock is nigh my love,
Her station is right my love,
Life is secure with Lady Jane.

The Indifferent

John Donne

     I can love both fair and brown,
Her whom abundance melts, and her whom want betrays,
Her who loves loneness best, and her who masks and plays,
    Her whom the country form'd, and whom the town,
      Her who believes, and her who tries,
      Her who still weeps with spongy eyes,
      And her who is dry cork and never cries;
I can love her, and her, and you, and you;
I can love any, so she be not true.

     Will no other vice content you?
Will it not serve your turn to do as did your mothers?
Or have you all old vices spent, and now would find out others?
    Or doth a fear that men are true torment you?
      O we are not; be not you so.
      Let me, and do you, twenty know.
      Rob me, but bind me not, and let me go.
Must I, who came to travail through you,
Grow your fix'd subject because you are true?

     Venus heard me sigh this song,
And by love's sweetest part, variety, she swore
She heard not this till now, and that it should be so no more.
    She went, examin'd, and return'd ere long,
      And said, "Alas, some two or three
      Poor heretics in love there be,
      Which think to 'stablish dangerous constancy,
But I have told them, 'Since you will be true,
You shall be true to them who're false to you.' "

14

The Cream

What makes a dangerous woman fascinating? The song, *Strange Brew,* and the accompanying poems by John Keats and Christopher Marlowe point up the question, but, fortunately, fail to answer it—fortunately, because if it ever were fully answered, we would lose an enduring source of inspiration for poetry and song.

Strange Brew was one of the most popular numbers of the *Cream,* an English rock group that disbanded just as they had almost begun to rival the *Beatles* and *Rolling Stones* in popularity. Notice how the song is qualified and strengethened by the sardonic humor, characteristic of so much British rock.

Strange Brew

Words and Music by Eric Clapton, Felix Pappalardi, and Gail Collins
The Cream, *Disraeli Gears*, Atco (S) 33-232

Strange brew's killin' what's inside of you.
She's a witch of trouble in electric blue
In her own mad mind she's in love with you, with you.
Now what'cha gonna do?
Strange brew's killin' what's inside of you.

She's some kind a demon messin' in the glue.
If you don't watch out it'll stick to you, to you.
What kinda fool are you?
Strange brew, killin' what's inside of you.

On a boat in the middle of a raging sea,
She would make a scene for it all to be ignored
And wouldn't you be bored?
Strange brew, killin' what's inside of you.

La Belle Dame Sans Merci

John Keats

Ah, what can ail thee, wretched wight,
 Alone and palely loitering;
The sedge is withered from the lake,
 And no birds sing.

Ah, what can ail thee, wretched wight,
 So haggard and so woe-begone?
The squirrel's granary is full,
 And the harvest's done.

I see a lily on thy brow,
 With anguish moist and fever dew;
And on thy cheek a fading rose
 Fast withereth too.

I met a lady in the meads
 Full beautiful, a faery's child;
Her hair was long, her foot was light,
 And her eyes were wild.

I set her on my pacing steed,
 And nothing else saw all day long;
For sideways would she lean, and sing
 A faery's song.

I made a garland for her head,
 And bracelets too, and fragrant zone;
She looked at me as she did love,
 And made sweet moan.

She found me roots of relish sweet,
 And honey wild, and manna dew;
And sure in language strange she said,
 I love thee true.

She took me to her elfin grot,
 And there she gazed and sighèd deep,
And there I shut her wild sad eyes–
 So kissed to sleep.

And there we slumber on the moss,
 And there I dreamed, ah woe betide,
The latest dream I ever dreamed
 On the cold hill side.

I saw pale kings, and princes too,
 Pale warriors, death-pale were they all;
Who cried–"La belle Dame sans merci
 Hath thee in thrall!"

I saw their starved lips in the gloam
 With horrid warning gapèd wide,
And I awoke, and found me here
 On the cold hill side.

Helen

from
The Tragical History of Doctor Faustus

Christopher Marlowe

Was this the face that launched a thousand ships,
And burned the topless towers of Ilium?–
Sweet Helen, make me immortal with a kiss!–
Her lips suck forth my soul: see where it flees!–
Come, Helen, come, give me my soul again.
Here will I dwell, for heaven is in these lips,
And all is dross that is not Helena.
I will be Paris, and for love of thee,
Instead of Troy, shall Wittenberg be sacked,
And I will combat with weak Menelaus,
And wear thy colours on my plumèd crest;
Yes, I will wound Achilles in the heel,
And then return to Helen for a kiss.
Oh, thou art fairer than the evening air
Clad in the beauty of a thousand stars;
Brighter art thou than flaming Jupiter
When he appeared to hapless Semele;
More lovely than the monarch of the sky
In wanton Arethusa's azured arms;
And none but thou shalt be my paramour!

15

Harry Nilsson

In Elizabethan times—the golden age of song—composers and lyricists labored long and carefully to free their songs from any impression of labor or care. The ideal was a song that flowed with such ease that the listener might think it composed on the spot, a playful ebullience of spontaneous wit and feeling. At the same time, however, the listener would be amazed at the intricate elegance of words and melody that accompanied the easy expression. Songs that achieved this paradoxical effect were said by critics to have "grace".

To what extent is "grace" found in the renaissance of song taking place today? At first we might think it non-existent, for now the language, thought, and feeling of song work for the common man instead of the courtly aristocrat, and elegance is to be avoided at all cost. Contemporary song, however, aims at a quality somewhat akin to the grace of Elizabethan lyric. As yet there is no good name for it, but what produces it is a seemingly effortless and yet perfect integration of casual expression with feelings appropriate to ordinary existence, an integration achieved by means of a few light strokes of musical and lyrical fancy. Few songwriters can match Harry Nilsson's mastery of this technique. Highly esteemed by his fellow artists, Nilsson compounds the effect of his "artful artlessness" by making his songs subtly suggestive as well as charming. In his song, *1941,* for example, he not only tells a good story, but also evokes the background of daily living, loving, and dying, speaking to us most movingly by what he does *not* say.

1941

Words and Music by Harry Nilsson
Pandemonium Shadow Show, RCA Victor LSP 3874

Well in 1941
    a happy father had a son,
And by 1944
    the father walks right out the door,
And in '45
    the mama and son were still alive,
But who could tell in '46
    if the two were to survive?

Well the years were passin' quickly
    but not fast enough for him,
So he closed his eyes 'til '55
    then he opened them again,
And he looked around and saw a clown
    And the clown seemed very gay,
And he said,
    "I'd like to join that circus clown and run away."

Well he followed every railroad track
    and every highway sign,
And he had a girl in each new town
    and the towns he left behind,
And the open road
    was the only road he knew,
But the color of his dream was slowly turning into blue.

Then he met a girl,
    the kind of girl he'd wanted all his life,
She was soft and kind and good to him,
    so he took her for his wife,
And they got a house not far from town
    and in a little while,
The girl had seen the doctor
    and she came home with a smile.

Now in 1961
    a happy father had a son,
And by 1964
    the father walks right out the door,
And in '65
    the mama and son were still around,
But what will happen to the boy when the circus comes to town?

anyone lived in a pretty how town

E. E. Cummings

anyone lived in a pretty how town
(with up so floating many bells down)
spring summer autumn winter
he sang his didn't he danced his did.

Women and men (both little and small)
cared for anyone not at all
they sowed their isn't they reaped their same
sun moon stars rain

children guessed (but only a few
and down they forgot as up they grew
autumn winter spring summer)
that noone loved him more by more

when by now and tree by leaf
she laughed his joy she cried his grief
bird by snow and stir by still
anyone's any was all to her

someones married their everyones
laughed their cryings and did their dance
(sleep wake hope then) they
said their nevers they slept their dream

stars rain sun moon
(and only the snow can begin to explain
how children are apt to forget to remember
with up so floating many bells down)

one day anyone died i guess
(and noone stooped to kiss his face)
busy folk buried them side by side
little by little and was by was

all by all and deep by deep
and more by more they dream their sleep
noone and anyone earth by april
wish by spirit and if by yes.

Women and men (both dong and ding)
summer autumn winter spring
reaped their sowing and went their came
sun moon stars rain

Without Her

Words and Music by Harry Nilsson
Pandemonium Shadow Show, RCA Victor LSP 3874

*I spend the night in the chair
  thinking she'll be there,
    but she never comes
      and then I wake up
        and wipe the sleep from my eyes
        and I rise
          to face another day
            without her.*

*It's just no good anymore
  when you walk through the door
    of an empty room
      and then you go inside
        and set a table for one;
        it's no fun
          when you spend a day
          without her.*

*We burst the pretty balloon –
  took us to the moon,
    such a beautiful thing,
      but it's empty now
        and it sounds like a lie
        if I say I'd rather die
          than live
            without her.*

*Love is a beautiful thing
  when it knows how to swing
    and it grooves like a clock
      but the hands on the clock
        tell the lovers to part
        and it's breakin' my heart
          to have to spend another day
            without her.*

*I spend the night in the chair
  thinking she'll be there
    but she never comes
      and then I wake up
        and wipe the sleep from my eyes
        and I rise
          to face another day
            without her.*

*Can't go on without her,
  there's no song without her,
    it's all wrong without her,
      can't go on without her . . .*

When the Lamp Is Shattered

Percy Bysshe Shelley

When the lamp is shattered
The light in the dust lies dead–
  When the cloud is scattered
The rainbow's glory is shed.
  When the lute is broken,
Sweet tones are remembered not;
  When the lips have spoken,
Loved accents are soon forgot.

  As music and splendour
Survive not the lamp and the lute,
  The heart's echoes render
No song when the spirit is mute:–
  No song but sad dirges,
Like the wind through a ruined cell,
  Or the mournful surges
That ring the dead seaman's knell.

  When hearts have once mingled
Love first leaves the well-built nest;
  The weak one is singled
To endure what it once possessed.
  O Love! who bewailest
The frailty of all things here,
  Why choose you the frailest
For your cradle, your home, and your bier?

  Its passions will rock thee
As the storms rock the ravens on high;
  Bright reason will mock thee,
Like the sun from a wintry sky.
  From thy nest every rafter
Will rot, and thine eagle home
  Leave thee naked to laughter,
When leaves fall and cold winds come.

So We'll Go No More A-Roving

George Gordon, Lord Byron

1
So we'll go no more a-roving
  So late into the night,
Though the heart be still as loving,
  And the moon be still as bright.

2
For the sword outwears its sheath,
  And the soul wears out the breast,
And the heart must pause to breathe,
  And Love itself have rest.

3
Though the night was made for loving,
  And the day returns too soon,
Yet we'll go more a-roving
  By the light of the moon.

16

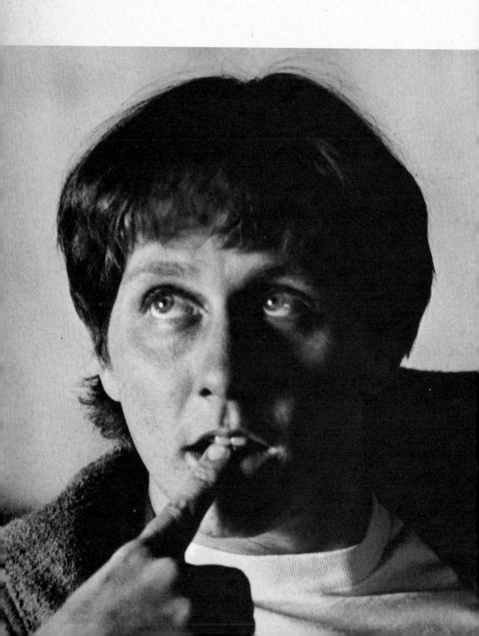

Bob Lind

To treat love lightly and yet truthfully is not an easy task for either a songwriter or a poet. There are always the dangers of sounding insincere or overly sentimental, of appearing artificial or uncontrolled. When heard in conjunction with his music, Bob Lind's lyrics for *Elusive Butterfly* seem to slip by these dangers with ease. Spenser, Shelley, and Shakespeare also try to project a distinct attitude toward love in the accompanying poems, and the reader might ask himself how they and Lind manage to hit just the note they are after and not another. Technically, the problem posed here is the management of *tone.*

Elusive Butterfly of Love

Words and Music by Bob Lind
Don't Be Concerned, World Pacific 77808

You might wake up some morning
         to the sound of something moving past your window in the wind.
And, if you're quick enough to rise,
         you'll catch the fleeting glimpse of someone's fading shadow.
Out on the new horizon,
         you may see the floating motion of a distant pair of wings.
And, if the sleep has left your ears,
         you might hear footsteps running through an open meadow.
Don't be concerned, it will not harm you,
         it's only me pursuing something I'm not sure of.
Across my dreams, with nets of wonder,
         I chase the bright, elusive butterfly of love.

You might have heard my footsteps,
         echo softly in the distance, through the canyons of your mind.
I might have even called your name
         as I ran searching for something to believe in.
You might have seen me running through the long,
         abandoned ruins of the dreams you left behind.
If you remember something there that glided past you
         followed close by heavy breathing,
Don't be concerned, it will not harm you,
         it's only me pursuing something I'm not sure of
Across my dreams, with nets of wonder,
         I chase the bright, elusive butterfly of love.

Manifestations of Tao

Laotse
(translated by Lin Yutang)

The marks of great Character
Follow alone from the Tao.

The thing that is called Tao
   Is elusive, evasive.
Evasive, elusive,
   Yet latent in it are forms.
Elusive, evasive,
   Yet latent in it are objects.
Dark and dim,
   Yet latent in it is the life-force.
The life-force being very true,
   Latent in it are evidences.

From the days of old till now
Its Named (manifested forms) have never ceased,
By which we may view the Father of All Things.
How do I know the shape of Father of All Things?
   Through These!

Lyke As a Huntsman

Edmund Spenser

Lyke as a huntsman after weary chace,
Seeing the game from him escapt away,
Sits downe to rest him in some shady place
With panting hounds beguiled of their pray:
So after long pursuit and vaine assay,
When I all weary had the chace forsooke,
The gentle deare returned the selfe-same way,
Thinking to quench her thirst at the next brooke.
There she beholding me with mylder looke,
Sought not to fly, but fearelesse still did bide:
Till I in hand her yet halfe trembling tooke,
And with her owne goodwill hir fyrmely tyde.
Strange thing me seemed to see a beast so wyld,
So goodly wonne with her owne will beguyld.

Love

Percy Bysshe Shelley

Why is it said thou canst not live
   In a youthful breast and fair,
Since thou eternal life canst give,
   Canst bloom for ever there?
Since withering pain no power possest,
   Nor age, to blanch thy vermeil hue,
Nor time's dread victor, death, confest
   Tho' bathed with his poison dew,
Still thou retain'st unchanging bloom,
Fixt tranquil, even in the tomb.
And oh! when on the blest reviving
   The day-star dawns of love,
Each energy of soul surviving
   More vivid, soars above,
Hast thou ne'er felt a rapturous thrill,
   Like June's warm breath, athwart thee fly,
O'er each idea then to steal,
   When other passions die?
Felt it in some wild noonday dream,
When sitting by the lonely stream,
Where Silence says, Mine is the dell;
   And not a murmur from the plain,
And not an echo from the fell,
   Disputes her silent reign.

17

Leonard Cohen

The lyrics of Leonard Cohen may be among the finest ever written in the English language. Independent of his music, most of them can stand as beautiful poems, demonstrative proof of the potential that the popular song has as an art form. Cohen has been known for some years now as a Canadian poet of great merit. His poetry and song-poems explore the farthest reaches of sexual and spiritual awareness.

We will forgo the temptation of "revealing" Cohen, and instead, refer readers to the lyrics themselves and four poems from the *Book of Tao,* written about 600 B.C. by Laotse, a gentle Chinese mystic who founded Taoism, one of the great Asian religions. Possibly Cohen never read Laotse's work. We draw upon it merely to illuminate the way of looking at life that Cohen seems to share with this ancient wise one. To prepare for the experience of Cohen's songs, the listener might also try to learn something about the Christian doctrines of grace, the role of "Earth Mother" in pagan fertility rites, and what a hell it is to be a creative artist.

The poems by Laotse and Alexander Pope that accompany *Teachers* represent attempts to answer the kind of question posed in that song. Pope's answers will possibly infuriate some readers, and Laotse's might be totally unacceptable to others. Why is this so?

Suzanne

Words and Music by Leonard Cohen
Songs of Leonard Cohen, Columbia CS 9533

Suzanne takes you down
To her place near the river
You can hear the boats go by
You can spend the night beside her.
And you know that she's half crazy
But that's why you want to be there
And she feeds you tea and oranges
That come all the way from China.
And just when you mean to tell her
That you have no love to give her
Then she gets you on her wavelength
And she lets the river answer
That you've always been her lover
And you want to travel with her
And you want to travel blind
And you know that she will trust you
For you've touched her perfect body
   with your mind.

And Jesus was a sailor
When he walked upon the water
And he spent a long time watching
From his lonely wooden tower.
And when he knew for certain
Only drowning men could see him
He said, "All men will be sailors then
Until the sea shall free them."
But he himself was broken
Long before the sky would open
Forsaken, almost human,
He sank beneath your wisdom like a stone.
And you want to travel with him
And you want to travel blind
And you think maybe you'll trust him
For he's touched your perfect body
   with his mind.

Now Suzanne takes your hand
And she leads you to the river
She is wearing rags and feathers
From Salvation Army counters.
And the sun pours down like honey
On our lady of the harbour;
And she shows you where to look
Among the garbage and the flowers.
There are heroes in the seaweed,
There are children in the morning,
They are leaning out for love
And they will lean that way forever.
While Suzanne holds the mirror
And you want to travel with her
And you want to travel blind
And you know that you can trust her
For she's touched your perfect body
   with her mind.

Peter Quince at the Clavier

Wallace Stevens

I

Just as my fingers on these keys
Make music, so the selfsame sounds
On my spirit make a music, too.

Music is feeling, then, not sound;
And thus it is that what I feel,
Here in this room, desiring you,

Thinking of your blue-shadowed silk,
Is music. It is like the strain
Waked in the elders by Susanna.

Of a green evening, clear and warm,
She bathed in her still garden, while
The red-eyed elders watching, felt

The basses of their beings throb
In witching chords, and their thin blood
Pulse pizzicati of Hosanna.

II

In the green water, clear and warm,
Susanna lay.

She searched
The touch of springs,
And found
Concealled imaginings.
She sighed,
For so much melody.

Upon the bank, she stood
In the cool
Of spent emotions.
She felt, among the leaves,
The dew
Of old devotions.

She walked upon the grass,
Still quavering.
The winds were like her maids,
On timid feet,
Fetching her woven scarves,
Yet wavering.

A breath upon her hand
Muted the night.
She turned–
A cymbal crashed,
And roaring horns.

III

Soon, with a noise like tambourines,
Came her attendant Byzantines.

They wondered why Susanna cried
Against the elders by her side;

And as they whispered, the refrain
Was like a willow swept by rain.

Anon, their lamps' uplifted flame
Revealed Susanna and her shame.

And then, the simpering Byzantines
Fled, with a noise like tambourines.

IV

Beauty is momentary in the mind–
The fitful tracing of a portal;
But in the flesh it is immortal.

The body dies; the body's beauty lives.
So evenings die, in their green going,
A wave, interminably flowing.
So gardens die, their meek breath scenting
The cowl of winter, done repenting.

So maidens die, to the auroral
Celebration of a maiden's choral.

Susanna's music touched the bawdy strings
Of those white elders; but, escaping,
Left only Death's ironic scraping.
Now, in its immortality, it plays
On the clear viol of her memory,
And makes a constant sacrament of praise.

Water

Laotse
(translated by Lin Yutang)

The best of men is like water;
  Water benefits all things
  And does not compete with them.
It dwells in (the lowly) places that all disdain—
  Wherein it comes near to the Tao.

In his dwelling, (the Sage) loves the (lowly) earth;
In his heart, he loves what is profound;
In his relations with others, he loves kindness;
In his words, he loves sincerity;
In government, he loves peace;
In business affairs, he loves ability;
In his actions, he loves choosing the right time.
  It is because he does not contend
  That he is without reproach.

The Spirit of the Valley

Laotse
(translated by Lin Yutang)

The Spirit of the Valley never dies.
It is called the Mystic Female.
  The Door of the Mystic Female
  Is the root of Heaven and Earth.

  Continuously, continuously,
  It seems to remain.
Draw upon it
And it serves you with ease.

Futility of Contention

Laotse
(translated by Lin Yutang)

To yield is to be preserved whole.
To be bent is to become straight.
To be hollow is to be filled.
To be tattered is to be renewed.
To be in want is to possess.
To have plenty is to be confused.

Therefore the Sage embraces the One,
And becomes the model of the world.
He does not reveal himself,
   And is therefore luminous.
He does not justify himself,
   And is therefore far-famed.
He does not boast of himself,
   And therefore people give him credit.
He does not pride himself,
   And is therefore the chief among men.

It is because he does not contend
That no one in the world can contend against him.

Is it not indeed true, as the ancients say,
   "To yield is to be preserved whole?"
Thus he is preserved and the world does him homage.

She Was a Phantom of Delight

William Wordsworth

She was a Phantom of delight
When first she gleamed upon my sight;
A lovely Apparition sent
To be a moment's ornament;
Her eyes as stars of Twilight fair;
Like Twilight's, too, her dusky hair;
But all things else about her drawn
From May-time and the cheerful Dawn;
A dancing Shape, an Image gay,
To haunt, to startle, and way-lay.

I saw her upon nearer view,
A Spirit, yet a Woman too!
Her household motions light and free,
And steps of virgin-liberty;
A countenance in which did meet
Sweet records, promises as sweet;
A Creature not too bright or good
For human nature's daily food;
For transient sorrows, simple wiles,
Praise, blame, love, kisses, tears and smiles.

And now I see with eye serene
The very pulse of the machine;
A Being breathing thoughtful breath,
A Traveller between life and death;
The reason firm, the temperate will,
Endurance, foresight, strength, and skill;
A perfect Woman, nobly planned,
To warn, to comfort, and command;
And yet a Spirit still, and bright
With something of angelic light.

Teachers

Words and Music by Leonard Cohen
Songs of Leonard Cohen, Columbia CS 9533

I met a woman long ago
Her hair the black that black can go;
"Are you a teacher of the heart?"
Soft she answered, "No."

I met a girl across the sea
Her hair the gold that gold can be;
"Are you a teacher of the heart?"
"Yes, but not for thee."

I met a man who lost his mind
In some lost place I had to find;
"Follow me," the wise man said
But he walked behind.

I walked into a hospital
Where none was sick and none was well.
When at night the nurses left
I could not walk at all.

Morning came and then came noon,
Dinner time, scalpel blade
Lay beside
My silver spoon.

Some girls wander by mistake
Into the mess that scapels make;
"Are you the teachers of my heart?"
"We teach old hearts to break."

One morning I woke up alone,
The hospital, the nurses gone;
"Have I carved enough, my lord?"
"Child, you are a bone."

I ate and ate and ate.
No, I did not miss a plate;
"Well, how much do these suppers cost?"
"We'll take it out in hate."

I spent my hatred every place
On every work, on every face;
Someone gave me wishes
And I wished for an embrace.

Several girls embraced me, then
I was embraced by men;
"Is my passion perfect?"
"No, do it once again."

I was handsome, I was strong,
I knew the words of every song;
"Did my singing please you?"
"No, the words you sang were wrong."

Who is it whom I address?
Who takes down what I confess?
"Are you the teachers of my heart?"
"We teach old hearts to rest."

"Teachers, are my lessons done?
I cannot do another one."
They laughed and laughed and said,
"Well, child, are your lessons done?
Are your lessons done?
Are your lessons done?"

The Bear on the Delhi Road

Earle Birney

Unreal, tall as a myth
by the road the Himalayan bear
is beating the brilliant air
with his crooked arms.
About him two men, bare,
spindly as locusts, leap.
One pulls on a ring
in the great soft nose; his mate
flicks, flicks with a stick,
up at the rolling eyes.

They have not led him here,
down from the fabulous hills
to this bald, alien plain
and the clamorous world, to kill
but simply to teach him to dance.

They are peaceful both, these spare
men of Kashmir, and the bear
alive is their living, too.
If far on the Delhi way
around him galvanic they dance
it is merely to wear, wear
from his shaggy body the tranced
wish forever to stay
only an ambling bear
four-footed in berries.

It is no more joyous for them
in this hot dust to prance
out of reach of the praying claws
sharpened to paw for ants
in the shadows of deodars.
It is not easy to free
myth from reality
or rear this fellow up
to lurch, lurch with them
in the tranced dancing of men.

What I Expected

Stephen Spender

What I expected was
Thunder, fighting,
Long struggles with men
And climbing.
After continual straining
I should grow strong;
Then the rocks would shake
And I should rest long.

What I had not forseen
Was the gradual day
Weakening the will
Leaking the brightness away,
The lack of good to touch
The fading of body and soul
Like smoke before wind
Corrupt, unsubstantial.

The wearing of Time,
And the watching of cripples pass
With limbs shaped like questions
In their odd twist,
The pulverous grief
Melting the bones with pity,
The sick falling from earth—
These, I could not foresee.

For I had expected always
Some brightness to hold in trust,
Some final innocence
To save from dust;
That, hanging solid,
Would dangle through all
Like the created poem
Or the dazzling crystal.

Rubaiyat of Omar Khayyam

Edward FitzGerald

(XXVII-XXXIV)

Myself when young did eagerly frequent
Doctor and Saint, and heard great argument
   About it and about; but evermore
Came out by the same door where in I went.

With them the seed of Wisdom did I sow,
And with mine own hand wrought to make it grow;
   And this was all the Harvest that I reaped—
"I came like Water, and like Wind I go."

Into this Universe, and *Why* not knowing,
Nor *Whence,* like Water willy-nilly flowing;
   And out of it, as Wind along the Waste,
I know not *Whither,* willy-nilly blowing.

What, without asking, hither hurried *Whence?*
And, without asking, *Whither* hurried hence!
   Oh, many a Cup of this forbidden Wine
Must drown the memory of that insolence!

Up from Earth's Centre through the Seventh Gate
I rose, and on the Throne of Saturn sate,
   And many a Knot unravel'd by the Road;
But not the Master-knot of Human Fate.

There was the Door to which I found no Key;
There was the Veil through which I might not see;
   Some little talk awhile of ME AND THEE
There was—and then no more of THEE AND ME.

Earth could not answer; nor the Seas that mourn
In flowing Purple, of their Lord forlorn;
   Nor rolling Heaven, with all his Signs reveal'd
And hidden by the sleeve of Night and Morn.

Then of the THEE IN ME who works behind
The Veil, I lifted up my hands to find
   A Lamp amid the Darkness; and I heard,
As from Without—"THE ME WITHIN THEE BLIND!"

Conquering the World By Inaction

Laotse
(translated by Lin Yutang)

The student of knowledge (aims at) learning day by day;
The student of Tao (aims at) losing day by day.
    By continual losing
    One reaches doing nothing.
    By doing nothing everything is done.
He who conquers the world often does so by doing nothing.
When one is compelled to do something,
The world is already beyond his conquering.

from

Essay on Man

Alexander Pope

Presumptuous Man! the reason wouldst thou find,
Why form'd so weak, so little, and so blind?
First, if thou canst, the harder reason guess,
Why form'd no weaker, blinder, and no less?
Ask of thy monther earth, why oaks are made
Taller or stronger than the weeds they shade?
Or ask of yonder argent fields above,
Why Jove's Satellites are less than Jove?
    Of Systems possible, if 'tis confest
That Wisdom infinite must form the best,
Where all must full or not coherent be,
And all that rises, rise in due degree;
Then, in the scale of reas'ning life, 'tis plain,
There must be, somewhere, such a rank as Man:
And all the question (wrangle e'er so long)
Is only this, if God has plac'd him wrong?
    Respecting Man, whatever wrong we call,
May, must be right, as relative to all.
In human works, tho' labour'd on with pain,
A thousand movements scarce one purpose gain;
In God's one single can its end produce;
Yet serves to second too some other use.
So Man, who here seems principal alone,
Perhaps acts second to some sphere unknown,
Touches some wheel, or verges to some goal;
'Tis but a part we see, and not a whole.

When the proud steed shall know why Man restrains
His fiery course, or drives him o'er the plains;
When the dull Ox, why now he breaks the clod,
Is now a victim, and now Egypt's God:
Then shall Man's pride and dulness comprehend
His actions', passions', being's, use and end;
Why doing, suff'ring, check'd, impell'd; and why
This hour a slave, the next a deity.
Then say not Man's imperfect, Heav'n in fault;
Say rather, Man's as perfect as he ought:
His knowledge measur'd to his state and place;
His time a moment, and a point his space.
If to be perfect in a certain sphere,
What matter, soon or late, or here or there?
The blest today is as completely so,
As who began a thousand years ago.

    • • •

Better for Us, perhaps, it might appear,
Were there all harmony, all virtue here;
That never air or ocean felt the wind;
That never passion discompos'd the mind.
But ALL subsists by elemental strife;
And Passions are the elements of Life.
The gen'ral Order, since the whole began,
Is kept in Nature, and is kept in Man.

    • • •

The bliss of Man (could Pride that blessing find)
Is not to act or think beyond mankind;
No pow'rs of body or of soul to share,
But what his nature and his state can bear.
Why has not Man a microscopic eye?
For this plain reason, Man is not a Fly.
Say what the use, were finer optics giv'n,
T' inspect a mite, not comprehend the heav'n?
Or touch, if trembling alive all o'er,
To smart and agonize at ev'ry pore?
Or quick effluvia darting thro' the brain,
Die of a rose in aromatic pain?
If nature thunder'd in his op'ning ears,
And stunn'd him with the music of the spheres,
How would he wish that Heav'n had left him still
The whisp'ring Zephyr, and the purling rill?
Who finds not Providence all good and wise,
Alike in what it gives, and what denies?

Cease then, nor ORDER Imperfection name:
Our proper bliss depends on what we blame.
Know thy own point: This kind, this due degree
Of blindness, weakness, Heav'n bestows on thee.
Submit.–In this, or any other sphere,
Secure to be as blest as thou canst bear:
Safe in the hand of one disposing Pow'r,
Or in the natal, or the mortal hour.
All Nature is but Art, unknown to thee;
All Chance, Direction, which thou canst not see;
All Discord, Harmony not understood;
All partial Evil, universal Good:
And, spite of Pride, in erring Reason's spite,
One truth is clear, WHATEVER IS, IS RIGHT.
     • • •
Ask of the Learn'd the way? The Learn'd are blind;
This bids to serve, and that to shun mankind;
Some place the bliss in action, some in ease,
Those call it Pleasure, and Contentment these;
Some sunk to Beasts, find pleasure end in pain;
Some swell'd to Gods, confess ev'n Virtue vain;
     • • •
Or indolent, to each extreme they fall,
To trust in ev'ry thing, or doubt of all.
   Who thus define it, say they more or less
Than this, that Happiness is Happiness?
   Take Nature's path, and mad Opinion's leave;
All states can reach it, and all heads conceive;
Obvious her goods, in no extreme they dwell;
There needs but thinking right, and meaning well;
And mourn our various portions as we please,
Equal is Common Sense, and Common Ease.

The Stranger Song

Words and Music by Leonard Cohen
Songs of Leonard Cohen, Columbia CS 9533

It's true that all men you knew
Were dealers who said they were through
With dealing every time you gave them shelter.
I know that kind of man;
It's hard to hold the hand of anyone
Who's reaching for the sky just to surrender—
Who's reaching for the sky just to surrender.

And then sweeping up the jokers that
*   he left behind,*
You find he did not leave you very much–
Not even laughter.
Like any dealer, he was watching for the card
*   that is so high and wild*
He'll never need to deal another.
He was just some Joseph looking for a
*   manger–*
He was just some Joseph looking for a
*   manger.*

And then leaning on your window sill,
He'll say one day you caused his will
To weaken with your love and warmth
*   and shelter*
And then taking from his wallet
*   an old schedule of trains, he'll say,*
"I told you when I came I was a stranger–
I told you when I came I was a stranger."

But now another stranger
Seems to want to ignore his dreams
As though they were the burden of some other.
O' you've seen that kind of man before,
His golden arm dispatching cards,
But now it's rusted from the elbow to
*   the finger.*
Yes, he wants to trade the game he knows
*   for shelter.*

You hate to watch another tired man
  lay down his hand, like he was
  giving up the holy game of poker,
And while he talks his dreams to sleep
You notice there's a highway that is
  curling up like smoke above his shoulder–
It's curling up like smoke above his shoulder.

You tell him to come in sit down
But something makes you turn around.
The door is open; you can't close your shelter;
You try the handle of the road.
It opens; do not be afraid.
It's you my love, you who are the stranger–
It is you my love, you who are the stranger.

Well, I've been waiting. I was sure
We'd meet between the trains we're waiting for.
I think it's time to board another.
Please understand, I never had a secret chart
To get me to the heart
Of this or any other matter.
When he talks like this
  you don't know what he's after.
When he speaks like this
  you don't know what he's after.

Let's meet tomorrow, if you choose,
Upon the shore, beneath the bridge
That they are building on some endless river.
Then he leaves the platform
For the sleeping car that's warm; you realize
He's only advertising one more shelter
And it comes to you; he never was a stranger
And you say, "OK, the bridge or someplace later."

And then sweeping up the jokers that
*   he left behind,*
You find he did not leave you very much,
Not even laughter.
Like any dealer, he was watching for the card
*   that is so high and wild*
He'll never need to deal another.
He was just some Joseph looking for a
*   manger—*
He was just some Joseph looking for a
*   manger.*

And then leaning on your window sill,
He'll say one day you caused his will
To weaken with your love and warmth
*   and shelter;*
And then taking from his wallet
*   an old schedule of trains, he'll say,*
"I told you when I came I was a stranger—
I told you when I came I was a stranger."

Human Condition

Thom Gunn

Now it is fog, I walk
Contained within my coat;
No castle more cut off
By reason of its moat;
Only the sentry's cough,
The mercenaries' talk.

The street lamps, visible,
Drop no light on the ground,
But press beams painfully
In a yard of fog around.
I am condemned to be
An individual.

In the established border
There balances a mere
Pinpoint of consciousness.
I stay, or start from, here:
No fog makes more or less
The neighbouring disorder.

Particular, I must
Find out the limitation
Of mind and universe,
To pick thought and sensation
And turn to my own use
Disordered hate or lust.

I seek, to break, my span.
I am my one touchstone.
This is a test more hard
Than any ever known.
And thus I keep my guard
On that which makes me man.

Much is unknowable.
No problem shall be faced
Until the problem is;
I, born to fog, to waste,
Walk through hypothesis,
An individual.

The Nameless Ones

Conrad Aiken

Pity the nameless, and the unknown, where
bitter in heart they wait on the stonebuilt stair,
bend to a wall, forgotten, the freezing wind
no bitterer than the suburbs of the mind;

who from an iron porch lift sightless eyes,
a moment, hopeless, to inflaming skies;
shrink from the light as quickly as from pain,
twist round a corner, bend to the wall again;

are to be seen leaning against a rail
by ornamental waters where toy yachts sail;
glide down the granite steps, touch foot to float,
hate, and desire, the sunlight on the boat;

explore a sullen alley where ash-cans wait,
symbols of waste and want, at every gate;
emerge in sun to mingle with the crowd,
themselves most silent where the world most loud;

anonymous, furtive, shadows in shadow hidden;
who lurk at the garden's edge like guests unbidden;
stare through the leaves with hate, yet wait to listen
as bandstand music begins to rise and glisten;

the fierce, the solitary, divine of heart,
passionate, present, yet godlike and apart;
who, in the midst of traffic, see a vision;
and, on a park bench, come to a last decision.

Sisters of Mercy

Words and Music by Leonard Cohen
Songs of Leonard Cohen, Columbia CS 9533

Oh, the Sisters of Mercy
They are not departed or gone.
They were waiting for me
When I thought that I just can't go on.
And they brought me their comfort
And later they brought me their song.
O, I hope you run into them
You who've been traveling so long.

Yes, you who must leave everything
That you cannot control.
It begins with your family
But soon it comes round to your soul.
Well, I've been where you're hanging,
I think I can see how you're pinned;
When you're not feeling holy
Your loneliness says that you've sinned.

They lay down beside me,
I made my confession to them.
They touched both my eyes
And I touched the dew on their hem.
If your life is a leaf
That the seasons tear off and condemn,
They will bind you with love
That is graceful and green as a stem.

When I left they were sleeping;
I hope you run into them soon.
Don't turn on the lights,
You can read their address by the moon;
And you won't make me jealous
If I hear that they sweetened your night
We weren't lovers like that
And besides it would still be all right.
We weren't lovers like that
And besides it would still be all right.

The Force That Through the Green Fuse Drives the Flower

Dylan Thomas

The force that through the green fuse drives the flower
Drives my green age; that blasts the roots of trees
Is my destroyer.
And I am dumb to tell the crooked rose
My youth is bent by the same wintry fever.

The force that drives the water through the rocks
Drives my red blood; that dries the mouthing streams
Turns mine to wax.
And I am dumb to mouth unto my veins
How at the mountain spring the same mouth sucks.

The hand that whirls the water in the pool
Stirs the quicksand; that ropes the blowing wind
Hauls my shroud sail.
And I am dumb to tell the hanging man
How of my clay is made the hangman's lime.

The lips of time leech to the fountain head;
Love drips and gathers, but the fallen blood
Shall calm her sores.
And I am dumb to tell a weather's wind
How time has ticked a heaven round the stars.

And I am dumb to tell the lover's tomb
How at my sheet goes the same crooked worm.

En Una Noche Oscura

Saint John of the Cross
(translated by Roy Cambell)

Upon a gloomy night,
With all my cares to loving ardours flushed,
(O venture of delight!)
With nobody in sight
I went abroad when all my house was hushed.

In safety, in disguise,
In darkness up the secret stair I crept,
(O happy enterprise!)
Concealed from other eyes,
When all my house at length in silence slept.

Upon a lucky night
In secrecy, inscrutable to sight,
I went without discerning
And with no other light
Except for that which in my heart was burning.

It lit and led me through
More certain than the light of noonday clear
To where One waited near
Whose presence well I knew,
There where no other presence might appear.

Oh night that was my guide!
Oh darkness dearer than the morning's pride,
Oh night that joined the lover
To the beloved bride
Transfiguring them each into the other.

Within my flowering breast
Which only for himself entire I save
He sank into his rest
And all my gifts I gave
Lulled by the airs with which the cedars wave.

Over the ramparts fanned
While the fresh wind was fluttering his tresses,
With his serenest hand
My neck he wounded, and
Suspended every sense with its caresses.

Lost to myself I stayed
My face upon my lover having laid
From all endeavour ceasing:
And all my cares releasing
Threw them among the lilies there to fade.

A Dead Man Asks for a Drink

St. Denys Garneau

(translated by F. R. Scott)

A dead man asks for a drink
The well no longer has as much water as one would imagine
Who will bring the answer to the dead man
The spring says my stream is not for him.

So look now all his maids are starting off
Each with a bowl for each a spring
To slake the thirst of the master
A dead man who asks for a drink.

This one collects in the depth of the nocturnal garden
The soft pollen which springs up from flowers
In the warmth which lingers on at the enclosure of night
She enlarges this flesh in front of him

But the dead man still is thirsty and asks for a drink

That one collects by the silver of moonlit meadows
The corollas that were closed by the coolness of evening
She makes of them a well-rounded bouquet
A soft heaviness cool on the mouth
And hurries to offer it to the master

But the dead man is thirsty and asks for a drink

Then the third and first of the three sisters
Hurries also into the fields
While there rises in the eastern sky
The bright menace of dawn
She gathers with the net of her golden apron
The shining drops of morning dew
Fills up a cup and offers it to the master

But still he is thirsty and asks for a drink.

Then morning breaks in its glory
And spreads like a breeze the light over the valley
And the dead man ground to dust
The dead man pierced by rays like a mist
Evaporates and dies
And even the memory of him has vanished from the earth.

Embracing the One

Laotse
(translated by Lin Yutang)

In embracing the One with your soul,
    Can you never forsake the Tao?
In controlling your vital force to achieve gentleness,
    Can you become like the new-born child?
In cleansing and purifying your Mystic vision,
    Can you strive after perfection?
In loving the people and governing the kingdom,
    Can you rule without interference?
In opening and shutting the Gate of Heaven,
    Can you play the part of the Female?
In comprehending all knowledge,
    Can you renounce the mind?

To give birth, to nourish,
To give birth without taking possession,
To act without appropriation,
To be chief among men without managing them–
This is the Mystic Virtue.

18

The Rev. F. D. Kirkpatrick and The Rev. Dr. Martin Luther King

According to the Zodiac, we are entering the Age of Aquarius, a time of new beginnings and new possibilities for joy. Traditionally, Aquarius is represented as the powerfully muscled water-bearer of the gods carrying the Urn of Minos, pouring blessings on those who are open to them and condemnation on the narrow-minded and selfish; the Age of Aquarius is supposed to initiate this distribution on a world-wide scale. One does not have to believe in astrology to sense a certain truth in this characterization of our era. And if the Aquarian myth is applied to what is happening in popular music, the picture is especially apt. Aquarius can be re-interpreted as the black man, whose urn pours out not water but the blues, nourishing the oppressed, chastizing the oppressors, and involving us in the life of the common man. There in essence is the story that has been unfolding in these volumes.

In this section, the work of the Rev. F. D. Kirkpatrick and the Rev. Dr. Martin Luther King brings these functions of the blues into sharp focus. The Rev. Kirkpatrick's song, *The Cities Are Burning,* though urban in content, is pure rural blues in style, expressing with frightening clarity the anger and frustration which Black America is barely able to keep under control. Dr. King's speech, *I Have a Dream,* ennunciates the vision of a better world that sustains the black man through his suffering and that lives in the very pain of his music. Between the Rev. Kirkpatrick's song and Dr. King's speech there are strong connections. Rural blues, and their distant cousin, the gospel song, reach out directly to the audience, inviting them to share, at a gut level, the emotions and thoughts being expressed. When blues and gospel songs work, the audience physically responds to the singer. They dance, clap hands, shout "amen," and discover in this dialogue a community of will and feeling. In Dr. King's speech, the elements of rhythm and structure which make that dialogue possible in blues and gospel singing are also present, magnificently so, for the message they carry is in fact the fullest

development of their function. His message, in brief, is his medium in its most beautiful form: the brotherhood of the singer with his audience—the basis of the blues and gospel song—is extended to the brotherhood of man.

There is another parallel between Dr. King's speech and the music of his people. At his best, the blues singer-composer creates spontaneously, echoing virbations that he releases both in himself and in his audience. The famous portion of Dr. King's *I Have A Dream* address reprinted here was composed in just this fashion. Speaking on August 27, 1963 to 250,000 people who had marched to Washington to demand "jobs and freedom" for black Americans, Dr. King was so moved by the reaction of his audience that he departed from his written text and created in *I Have A Dream* what is in effect a great rhetorical poem. His wife, Mrs. Coretta King, gives this account:

"When he got to the rhythmic part of demanding freedom *now,* and jobs *now,* the crowd caught the timing and shouted "now!" in a cadence. Their response lifted Martin in a surge of emotion. Abandoning his written speech, he spoke from his heart, his voice soaring magnificently out over that great crowd and to all the world." *(Life,* Sept. 12, 1969, pp. 61-62.)

The Rev. Frederick Douglas Kirkpatrick was one of Dr. King's lieutenants in the civil rights struggle and during the Resurrection City demonstration of the poor in Washington, he won fame as the man who kept the demonstrators singing through the long ordeal of their encampment there. To hear an angrier statement of the emotions expressed in his song, *The Cities Are Burning,* one should listen, on the same Broadside album, to the song of his young partner, Jimmy Collier: *Burn, Baby, Burn.*

Also included here is the Rev. Kirkpatrick's song, *I'm Going Home on the Morning Train*—an example of how easily the form of the gospel song can be made to express the cause of freedom.

The Cities are Burning

Words and Music by the Rev. Frederick Douglass Kirkpatrick
Everybody's Got a Right to Live, Broadside BR 308
Hear also, *Pete Seeger Now*, Columbia CS 9717

Lord, you know these cities are burning
All over the U.S.A. Yes–

    These cities are burning now
    All over the U.S.A.
    Yes, you know if these white folks don't settle pretty soon
    We all goin' to wake up in Judgment Day.

You know, God told Noah about it–
'Bout a rainbow sign
There'll be no more water
But there'll be fire the next time.

    The Bible's fulfillin' now
    All over the U.S.A.
    Yes, you know if these white folks don't settle up soon–the U.S.A.–
    We all goin' to wake up in Judgment Day.
        Yeah!

You know, the first was in Los Angeles
In a section they call Watts
Then Newark, New Jersey, New York, and eighty more cities
All began to rock.

    Those cities are burning
    All over the U.S.A.
    Yes, you know if these white folks don't settle up soon
    We all goin' to wake up in Judgment Day.

You know Our Father which art in Heaven
White man owned me a hundred dollars
And he didn't give me but seven
Hallowed be Thy Name, Thy–Kingdom come
Hadn't taken that seven
You know I wouldn't have got none.

    That's why these cities are burning
    All over the U.S.A.
    The only solution I see to this whole thing
    Is non-violence through Martin Luther King.

I'm Going Home on the Morning Train

Words and Music by the Rev. Frederick Douglass Kirkpatrick
Everybody's Got a Right to Live, Broadside BR 308

*This song makes me remember when I was
just a lad of a boy. I used to sit around
in the evening time and listen to my mother
tell stories about the slave days.
Tears used to form in her eyes. I was too
young to know what she was crying about.
I used to hear her sing this song, "I'm
Going home on the Morning Train." And
early in the morning she'd get up and
sing this song:*

> *I'm going home on the morning train
> I'm going home on the morning train
> Evenin' train oh will be too late
> I'm going home on the morning train.*

*My old mother used to tell these stories.
She was born in Alabama and raised in
Mississippi. They used to pick cotton
on hot summer days when sometimes it
looked like the rows would be a mile and
a half long. Sometimes a bird would fly
over and they'd look up at the bird and
you would hear an old slave say, "Swing
low, sweet chariot, comin' to carry me
home." And sometimes late in the evenin'
an echo out of the woods would come,
from the grassy swamp, and an old slave
would say, "My Lord is callin' me–
callin' thru the thunder, trumpet
sounds within my soul, I AIN'T GOT LONG
TO STAY HERE." And after this was over,
I hear my mother sing:*

> *I'm going home on the morning train
> I'm going home on the morning train
> Evenin' train oh will be too late
> I'm going home on the morning train.*

*People used to be great church goers. On
a Sunday morning you'd see them coming
from miles around. They'd step inside this
little old wooden church out in the hills.*

*That old-fashioned preacher would take
his text. Sometimes before he took his
text you'd hear him sing a hymn, "Nearer
My God To Thee." After he was through singing
that old hymn he'd preach a sermon, and
after he finished preaching that sermon he'd
take up collection and say:*

> *Get right, church, and let's go home
> Get right, church, and let's go home
> Get right, church, oh, get right, church
> Get right, church, and let's go home.*

*You know, funeral services were great big
things in those days. A neighbor would die
and you'd see people coming from miles
around. They'd put up that casket in the
middle of that old wooden church. The
preacher would begin to preach the funeral
sermon on that Sunday morning. After he
finished preachin' the funeral, he'd send that
brother on up to heaven, and then he'd say:*

> *Back, back, hearse, and get your load
> Back, back, hearse, and get your load
> Back, back, hearse, oh, back, back, hearse
> Back, back, hearse and get your load.*

Looka here:

> *White folks, you can't stop us now
> White folks, you can't stop us now
> White folks, you can't, you can't,
>   white folks you can't, you can't
> White folks, you can't stop us now.*

Tell you what we're gonna do:

> *Organize, then we goin' home
> Organize, then we goin' home
> White folks be surprised
>   when they find us organized
> Organize, then we goin' home.*

> *I'm going home on the morning train
> I'm going home on the morning train
> Evenin' train, oh'll, be too late
> I'm going home on the morning train.*

from

I Have a Dream

By the Rev. Dr. Martin Luther King, Jr.
The March on Washington — The Official Album,
(available from Radio Station WRVR, 490 Riverside Drive,
New York 27, New York)

*I say to you today, my friends, that in spite of the difficulties
and frustrations of the moment I still have a dream. It is a dream
deeply rooted in the American dream.*

*I have a dream that one day this nation will rise up and live
out the true meaning of its creed: "We hold these truths to be
self-evident; that all men are created equal."*

*I have a dream that one day on the red hills of Georgia the
sons of former slaves and the sons of former slaveowners will be
able to sit down together at the table of brotherhood.*

*I have a dream that one day even the state of Mississippi, a
desert state sweltering with the heat of injustice and oppression,
will be transformed into an oasis of freedom and justice.*

*I have a dream that my four little children will one day live
in a nation where they will not be judged by the color of their
skin but by the content of their character.*

I have a dream today.

*I have a dream that one day the state of Alabama, whose
governor's lips are presently dripping with the words of interposition
and nullification, will be transformed into a situation where little
black boys and black girls will be able to join hands with little
white boys and white girls and walk together as sisters and brothers.*

I have a dream today.

*I have a dream that one day every valley shall be exalted,
every hill and mountain shall be made low, the rough places will
be made plain, and the crooked places will be made straight, and
the glory of the Lord shall be revealed, and all flesh shall see it
together.*

This is our hope. This is the faith with which I return to the South. With this faith we will be able to hew out of the mountain of despair a stone of hope. With this faith we will be able to transform the jangling discords of our nation into a beautiful symphony of brotherhood. With this faith we will be able to work together, to pray together, to struggle together, to go to jail together, to stand up for freedom together, knowing that we will be free one day.

This will be the day when all of God's children will be able to sing with new meaning

My country, 'tis of thee,
Sweet land of liberty,
    Of thee I sing:
Land where my fathers died,
Land of the pilgrims' pride,
From every mountain-side
    Let freedom ring.

And if America is to be a great nation this must become true. Se let freedom ring from the prodigious hilltops of New Hampshire.

Let freedom ring from the mighty mountains of New York.

Let freedom ring from the heightening Alleghenies of Pennsylvania!

Let freedom ring from the snowcapped Rockies of Colorado!

Let freedom ring from the curvacious peaks of California!

But not only that; let freedom ring from Stone Mountain of Georgia!

Let freedom ring from Lookout Mountain of Tennessee!

Let freedom ring from every hill and molehill of Mississippi. From every mountainside, let freedom ring.

When we let freedom ring, when we let it ring from every village and every hamlet, from every state and every city, we will be able to speed up that day when all of God's children, black men and white men, Jews and Gentiles, Protestants and Catholics, will be able to join hands and sing in the words of the old Negro spiritual, "Free at last! free at last! thank God almighty, we are free at last!"

About the Poets
Prepared especially for
secondary school students
by Kenneth J. Weber

Conrad Aiken (b. 1889)
is an American whose writings
include poetry, novels, short
stories, and literary criticism.
His work often shows a preoc-
cupation with music, and with
psychoanalysis.

Matthew Arnold (1822-1888)
is justly famous for his prose
works, and for his accomplished
literary criticism. In both areas,
he constantly argued against
materialism, selfishness, and
ugliness. As professor of poetry
at Oxford, and later as Inspector of Schools, he exerted a
considerable influence on the
English education system during
the nineteenth century. His
poetry is often filled with tones
of pessimism, and although
the craftsmanship is excellent,
it seldom reaches the poetic
heights attained by other nineteenth century writers such as
Browning or Tennyson.

Wystan Hugh Auden (b. 1907)
is an English-born American
poet and scholar who toyed with
Marxism in the 1930's, but has
become less politically radical
since. His poetry is intellectual
and marked by sharp and witty
observations of our society.

Robert Lawrence Binyon (1869-1943)
was born in England and
educated at Oxford. Binyon,
during his lifetime, was a renowned authority on Asiatic art.
His awareness of artistic qualities is very evident in his writing.

Alfred Earle Birney (b. 1904),
famous as a poet and as a
humorist, is a Canadian professor of English known for the
strong sense of irony in his
writing. His references and
imagery are very much those
of the Canadian physical and
cultural environment.

William Blake (1757-1827),
a mystic whose poetry is filled
with images of intense feeling,
was appalled by the creeping
materialism of his age and
sought a hopeful alternative in
visionary religion. Generally
considered a pre-Romantic or
early Romantic, he is in many
ways like early twentieth-cen-
tury poets in style and content.

George Gordon, Lord Byron (1788-1824)
might be the one poet
in English literary history
whose biography is read as
frequently as his poetry. A
wealthy and handsome man, he
stirred up such gossip in England that he eventually left for
the Continent. Although Byron
once said of his own poetry that
"No one has done more through
negligence to corrupt the language," any flaws in his poetry
are probably the result of over-
whelming energy.

John Clare (1793-1864)
was an English poet whose many
writings on the country and
country life have caused him to
be called, by some critics, the
English Robert Burns.

E. E. Cummings (1894-1962)
was an American who won early
attention as a painter and
draughtsman in Europe. What
would otherwise be simple satire
is given a special dimension in
his poetry through the use of
unusual syntax, typography, and
word combinations.

Stephen Crane (1871-1900),
an American, is known primarily
as a novelist, and particularly
for his novel *The Red Badge of
Courage.* Throughout his brief
career as a war correspondent
and writer, he suffered from both
ill health and malicious gossip.

The style of his poetry is clipped and cryptic, more in the modern vein than in the Victorian.

Emily Dickinson (1830-1886) is perhaps the best known woman poet of America. Although she led a secluded, quiet life in New England, her poetry was ahead of its time in conception and technique. Much of her poetry is characterized by a delightful and unusual use of ordinary language. Her poetry, which seems so relevant today, remained generally unpublished during her lifetime.

John Donne (1573-1631) was an English poet of the Metaphysical school. His career ranged from what we now know as the civil service to the ministry. Donne's poetry presents a strange mixture of theology and human love, in a style that is distinguished by its use of grandiose metaphors.

Sir Edward Dyer (c. 1550-1607) is one of the group of poets associated with Spenser, but was overshadowed by the latter's greatness. Dyer's poetry reflects the chivalry, imagery, and grace of the period, but often betrays a certain strain in an attempt to achieve an effect of beauty.

Edward FitzGerald (1809-1883) will be remembered for what is still regarded as the best translation of *The Rubaiyat of Omar Khayyam,* although the majority of his work was overshadowed by other "greats" of the Victorian era. FitzGerald used several translations of *The Rubaiyat* (in several languages) to create a work that captures better than any other the spirit of the Persian philosopher-poet.

St. Denys Garneau (1912-1943) was a prominent figure in French Canadian literature of the early twentieth century. Given to solitude and reflectiveness in his personal life, his work frequently touches on such subjects as death, loneliness, sadness, and silence.

Oliver Goldsmith (1728-1774) is perhaps better known for a novel, *The Vicar of Wakefield,* and a play, *She Stoops to Conquer,* than for his poetry. Despite the fact that he is generally associated with humorous writing, Goldsmith's work shows a real depth of perception and a profound awareness of human shortcomings.

Thomas Gunn (b. 1929) was educated at Cambridge and has lived for some time in California. His work is contemporary both in content and in idiom. He is well known for his series of poems that mythologizes the black-jacketed motorcycle rider wandering the country in search of meaningful values.

Robert Earl Hayden (b. 1913) is an American poet and university professor. Hayden has won an impressive number of awards for his poetry. Besides his own books, he frequently writes for magazines like *The Atlantic Monthly.*

Carl Moses Holman (b. 1919) was born in Mississippi. He is a graduate of Lincoln University and the University of Chicago, where he received an M.A. in 1944 as well as the Fiske Poetry Prize. He is now a member of the English faculty at Hampton Institute in Virginia.

James Langston Hughes (1902-1967) was one of the most popular black American poets of this century. His style is distinguished by his ability to create an atmosphere of tenderness and quiet pathos. Yet, he can also create images that repel and frighten when dealing with the plight of American black people.

Robinson Jeffers (1887-1962), an American born into a wealthy family, earned degrees in medicine and forestry. Jeffers moved his family to California where he built a house and a tower to ensure privacy and seclusion. His writing often reveals a sense of pessimism and frustration.

Donald Jeffrey (b. 1904) was born in Raleigh, North Carolina. A musician, professional singer, and social worker, he has been published in numerous anthologies.

Saint John of the Cross (1542-1591) was a Spanish mystic and founder of a branch of the Carmelite order. His mystic poetry and theological treatises have had a significant effect on modern Catholic thought.

Samuel Johnson (1709-1784), the famous Dr. Johnson, is regarded as the leading literary figure of a literary age. Famous for many things — his criticism, his politics, his dictionary — Johnson's first success in his career was achieved in poetry. His poetry, technically exact, is capable of savage pessimism and severe criticism.

John Keats (1795-1821) wrote his own epitaph: "Here lies one whose name was writ in water." His poetry is melancholy and haunted with a sad beauty. His life was a succession of sorrows — he lost his brother

to consumption; learned that he had it himself; and was rejected by his fiancée — all within a few short years. Although Keats was criticized severely in his first years as a poet, few other writers have left such a legacy of highly reputed works. Sensuous, passionate, concrete in detail and imagery, yet suggestive in emotion and atmosphere, his poetry is probably the most romantic of the Romantics.

Henry King (1592-1669) was bishop of Chichester and a close friend of Donne and Jonson. Although he is a minor figure in comparison with his friends, King's graceful verse ranks high in quality with that of his contemporaries.

Martin Luther King (1929-1968) was a black American clergyman and civil rights leader; winner of the Nobel Peace Prize in 1964 for his policies of nonviolence and resistance to segregation. Martin Luther King ranks among history's greatest fighters for justice and freedom, both for his qualities as a man, and for his abilities as a writer and leader.

Laotse (b.c. 604 B.C.) was a Chinese philosopher and the legendary founder of Taoism. Broadly, to follow the Tao, man gives up all his striving; his thoughts are of escaping from the illusions of desire through mystical contemplation.

Denise Levertov (b. 1923) was born in England but became a U.S. citizen in 1956. She has been called an "avant-garde" poet by some critics. Her own statements regarding poetry include the following. "Insofar as poetry has a social function, it is to awaken sleepers by other means than shock," and "I do not believe that a violent imitation of the horrors of our time is the concern of poetry . . . ."

Karen Lindsay (b. 1945)
was born in Hollywood, California. Her poetry has been published in *Kauri, Bardic Echoes, American Bard,* and *American Haiku.*

Richard Lovelace (c. 1618-1657)
is remembered for his Cavalier name, his military virtues, and two chivalric poems. Much of Lovelace's work lacks vigor, but in *To Lucasta* and *To Althea From Prison,* he had the perfect chivalric occasion and rose to it.

Walter Lowenfels (b. 1897)
was born and lives in New York State. Lowenfels has not only written a great deal of poetry himself, but has done considerable academic research on other poets as well.

Archibald MacLeish (b. 1892)
is an American lawyer who fought in the Spanish Civil War, helped plan UNESCO, edited *Fortune Magazine,* and lectured at Harvard. Much of MacLeish's writing is concerned with man's attempts to find himself in the vastness and complexity of the universe. His own life reflects such an attempt as well.

Christopher Marlowe (1564-1593)
is recognized as the one man who might have rivalled Shakespeare, but he was murdered in a tavern brawl before his career had reached its peak. He was a true Renaissance man, with his delving into both sensual and spiritual experience. Part of Marlowe's genius lay in the rhetorical power of his blank verse.

Kenneth McRobbie (b. 1929),
a Canadian who, besides his creative writing, has done considerable research into education and educational theory. He titled one of his collections "poems for the missile age."

John Milton (1608-1674)
was a Puritan, and a supporter of Cromwell, but believed in individual, civil, and religious liberty for everyone. Although his epic, *Paradise Lost,* would alone guarantee his fame, Milton's excellence extends to odes, pastorals, elegies, sonnets, and poetic drama.

Thomas Nashe (1567-1601)
was an active political writer as well as a poet. He campaigned vigorously against the Puritans in Elizabethan England.

Sir Henry John Newbolt (1862-1938)
studied for the law in England, but his love for literature led him to a career of writing and literary criticism. His novels have been forgotten, but his poetry will be remembered for its heartiness and optimism. Newbolt's schooling, his way of life, and his writing, all mark him as a conventional upper-class Englishman of the days of Empire.

Alden Nowlan (b. 1933)
was born in Nova Scotia. Nowlan's poetry deals with people and especially with people and life in small towns. His writing stresses the point that people are the same all over the world.

Seumas O'Sullivan (b. 1879)
is the pen name of James

Starkey. O'Sullivan has published several volumes of verse, most of which deals with the life and the myths of the Irish people. He was born in Dublin.

Wilfred Owen (1893-1918)
is most famous for his strong, occasionally vicious anti-war poetry, which ran counter to the highly patriotic feeling predominant during World War I, as expressed by such poets as Rudyard Kipling. He gave the fighting man's point of view instead of the homefront patriot's. He was killed just a week before the armistice. Owen is very like modern lyricists both in the strength of his feelings and the elliptical quality of his style. He frequently uses assonance rather than rhyme.

Uta Peikert (b. 1950)
was born in Berlin, but as a child moved to Canada with her family. Her contribution to this volume was written when she was seventeen, in high school.

Alexander Pope (1688-1744),
as a Roman Catholic, had enemies in eighteenth century England. And because he was a cripple, Pope was understandably a bitter man. This bitterness was given vent in elegant irony and brilliant satire. The balance and antithesis in his rhyming couplets has never been equalled.

Dudley Randall (b. 1914)
is an American poet who does not shy away from controversy. Among his works is an edition of poems dedicated to the late Malcolm X.

Edwin Arlington Robinson (1869-1935)
was an American whose skill in character portraits is well known. His poetry is marked by its economy, and surprising irony and humor. Robinson, quite late in career, was rescued from obscurity by President Theodore Roosevelt.

Vernon Scannell (b. 1922)
was born in Lincolnshire, England. His varied occupations — professional boxer, teacher of English, broadcaster, soldier, and freelance writer — have provided him with background for his writings. Scannel has published both poetry and prose, and is a fellow of the Royal Society of Literature. Scannel describes himself politically as a "romantic radical."

Penelope Schafer
kown professionally only as "Penelope," was born in Victoria, British Columbia, and has lived in Halifax, Vancouver, and Toronto. Her activities include public relations work for the Toronto *Telegram* and *Canadian Art*; writing pop lyrics and radio scripts for the Canadian Broadcasting Corporation; managing a rock band; writing and acting in a feature film, *Zero, the Fool;* and reading poetry at the Mariposa Festival and universities throughout Ontario.

William Shakespeare (1564-1616)
composed poetry of such brilliance and vitality that even if he had not produced a single play he would still be renowned today.

Percy Bysshe Shelley (1792-1822)
is a classic example of the Romantic and social rebel; even Shelley's death by drowning came about partially as an

act of defiance. Elaborate yet beautiful imagery characterizes his poetry, as he attempts to express spiritual qualities. Shelley tries to speak directly to the heart of his reader, and the consequent lack of precision occasionally leads to obscurity. Nevertheless, his poetry is a testament to the spontaneity and imagination in which he believed.

Sir Philip Sidney (1554-1586), a soldier, diplomat, poet, and critic, was trusted with government business in many countries on the Continent. After Sidney's death in battle (in Holland) Spenser extolled him in the poem *Astrophel.* Sidney was looked upon by his contemporaries as a model of chivalry.

Raymond Souster (b. 1912) is a Toronto banker and poet who is known for his witty use of everyday speech. His work frequently takes the form of short vignettes or lyrical portraits.

Stephen Spender (b. 1909), a very politically concerned intellectual and poet, often expresses disenchantment with English society. His poetry has immediacy and urgency, and is made particularly vivid through his use of imagery from technology.

Edmund Spenser (1552-1599), an early Elizabethan, is looked upon as one of the fathers of English poetry. His writing is chiefly on the subjects of religion, love, and morality, and is presented in verse that is filled with pictorial images. Spenser's handling of sound and rhythm gives his poems a musical quality all their own.

William Stafford (b. 1914) is an American university professor who is held in very high regard for his literary criticism.

Wallace Stevens (1879-1955) is renowned for his poetic technique. His poetry is evidence of the thinking of a religious sceptic, and is filled with suggestive detail written in what is often extravagant language.

Algernon Charles Swinburne (1837-1909) stirred up controversy by rejecting both the ethical and religious ideas of Victorian England. His verse flows like the melody of song and is rich in imagery and detail. Much of his inspiration came from the literature and mythology of ancient Greece and Rome.

Alfred, Lord Tennyson (1809-1892) was the poetic voice for Victorian sentiment. His great skill was in his use of imitative harmony and imagery. Unlike many other poets, he was probably more famous during his lifetime than after. As the mores of Victorian life fell into disrepute, Tennyson, their spokesman, fell with them.

Dylan Thomas (1914-1953), a literary hero of the twentieth century, is attractive to all students of poetry if only for his life style. He freely questioned and often rejected premises about life and art that to him had become mere dust-covered doctrines. He was born in Wales, and the effect of the beautiful, and ugly, aspects of the Welsh countryside is obvious in his work. Thomas' work is already a landmark in English literary history, because of its vigor and spontaneity. Vivid, often violent juxtapositions of images move the reader into sharing an emotional experience. His poetry, when read aloud, provokes an excitement which only a few poets in the English language have equalled.

Chidiock Tichborne (1558-1586)

was a political conspirator executed for his part in a plot to depose Queen Elizabeth I and put Mary Queen of Scots on the throne. His poem in this volume was written in the Tower of London the night before his death.

Judi Vyse (b. 1950),

a Canadian, is now attending the University of Toronto. Her poem in this volume was written when she was 16.

Vernon P. Watkins (b. 1906)

was born in Wales and uses some of the Welsh legends, but he is basically an English poet in the English tradition. He is at his best in his ballads which are filled with concrete imagery.

Charles Wesley (1707-1788)

was born in England and educated at Oxford. He is generally associated with his brother John, the founder of Methodism. Charles Wesley was the most voluminous hymn writer in the English language. The idiom and imagery of his hymns are quite traditional in nature.

Walt Whitman (1819-1892),

a robust, uninhibited poet, was in constant difficulty with his contemporaries. With his aggressive style, Whitman spoke as interpreter of life and prophet of America's greatness. His influence on subsequent American poets has been profound.

William Wordsworth (1770-7850),

co-author with Samuel Taylor Coleridge of the famous *Lyrical Ballads,* is often considered the father of the Romantic movement in poetry. Wordsworth's work has been both praised and damned. Although it is generally philosophical, it lacks the melody and grace of the other Romantic poets. He is at his best in his lyrical celebrations of nature.

Yevgeny Alexandrovich Yevtushenko (b. 1933)

was born in Siberia. Yevtushenko has gained fame for his poetic skill, and particularly for his ability to appeal to youth. His social themes and independent spirit often provoke unfriendly government reaction.

Suggestions for Study
Prepared especially for
secondary school students
by Kenneth J. Weber

Section 1: Bukka White and Traditional Blues
1. Explain why the stark simplicity of both *Joe Turner* and *You Don't
   Know My Mind* is such a strong factor in suggesting far more than
   the words of the songs actually state.
2. After hearing *Fixing to Die,* compare it with Tichborne's *Elegy.*
   What does the music add?

Section 2: John KaSandra and Urban Blues
Mose
1. What is your own emotional reaction to Mose? Try to outline what
   it is in *Mose* that causes your reaction.
2. In this unit, what is each writer's purpose?
3. Does this combination of poems suggest that the effect of poverty
   changes, or remains the same, in different locales and at different
   points in history?
   Don't Pat Me on the Back and Call Me Brother
4. Can you recognize the "three kinds of poetic truth" (outlined in the
   introduction to this section) in *Don't Pat Me on the Back . . .* ?
5. Examine some of the blues songs in this section, and in other
   sections of this book. Try to discover what features make the blues
   such a distinctive form.

Section 3: Woody Guthrie
Tom Joad
1. What are the various means by which Guthrie evokes pathos in
   Tom Joad?
2. Contrast one very personal selection from this unit with a selection
   that is more general. In your opinion, which one is more powerful?
   Why?
3. Is "the language of the people" more convincing than deliberately
   poetic language? Is there such a thing as "deliberately poetic
   language"? Support your opinions by reference to selections from
   this unit.
   Hard Travelin'
4. With the exception of Whitman's *Song of the Open Road,* all the
   works in this unit express a common theme.
   a) Identify this common theme.
   b) Explain how the lyrics, and each of the poems, present a variation
   of the theme.
   c) To what extent is Whitman's poem a satisfactory answer to the
   other selections in this unit?

Section 4: Ewan MacColl
The Ballad of the Carpenter
1. a) Is *The Ballad of the Carpenter* irreverent?
   b) What religious features does it share with *For Easter Sunday*?
   What poetic features?
   The First Time Ever I Saw Your Face
2. Which works in this unit do you believe (if any)? Why?

Section 5: Phil Ochs
Crucifixion
1. Examine other songs by Phil Ochs and compare them with the impact and techniques of *Crucifixion*.
2. Compare Ochs with other sharply satirical writers like Tom Lehrer. What are some of the differences in style and approach? Is there a relationship between the bitterness of the satire and the effectiveness of the poem?
3. Compare Whitman's attitude in his eulogy for Lincoln with Ochs' attitude in *Crucifixion*.
4. Add to this section by preparing a brief anthology, either of critical poetry, or of elegies.

Section 7: Jacques Brel
The Dove
1. Which work is more realistic, Owen's *The Send-Off* or Brel's *The Dove*? Which has the more powerful impact? What does realism contribute to that impact?
2. If the incident described in *Arms and the Boy* could be portrayed in large colored photographs, which would have a more lasting impact, the pictures, or the poem? Why is this so?
3. a) Would Scannel's *Walking Wounded* have been just as effective in prose?
   b) Is it really poetry?

Section 8: Malvina Reynolds
Little Boxes
1. a) What has caused the dehumanization that the works in this unit deplore?
   b) Do any of the works present any hope for salvation from the plastic world?
   What Have They Done to the Rain?
2. While examining the lyric and each of the poems in this unit, consider the following question: Does mankind *really believe* that the world will end?
3. How is the grass treated symbolically in each of the selections in this unit? (If you are able to view the film *The Persistent Seed*, produced by the National Film Board of Canada, compare the techniques of film statement with poetic and lyric statement.)

Section 9: Bruce MacKay
The Half-Masted Schooner
1. a) To what degree is each selection in this unit an expression of escape?
   b) To what degree is each an expression of a desire for freedom?
   c) Try to judge whether the imagery of each selection leads you more strongly to *i*) escape or *ii*) freedom.
   Sacraments of Evil
2. Bruce MacKay has made a film of *The Half-Masted Schooner*, in which he attempts to give a visual expression of both the imagery and the social comment in his lyric. (Produced by the National Film Board of Canada as an experimental film which MacKay calls a "musicfilm".) Try to present in 8mm film, or slide pictures, or photographs, or even pictures from magazines, a visual expression of *Sacraments of Evil*, or any other of the poems in the unit.

Song of the Black Veils

3. Whereas war poems so often point out the horrors of war, the selections in this unit share a somewhat different theme. What is the theme of each work presented here?
4. a) Binyon's *For the Fallen* was written with serious intent as a eulogy for dead soldiers. Does juxtaposing it with such poems as *To the Glorious Dead* and *Notes for a Movie Script* make a mockery of it? Explain your answer.
   b) What is the effect on *To Lucasta, On Going to the Wars* when it is juxtaposed with *To the Glorious Dead* and *Notes on a Movie Script*?

Section 10: David Crosby
Mind Gardens

1. Compare the outlook on solitude and isolation held by each of the writers in this section. (Check the biographies of the poets to see if their cultural environments might have affected their views.)
2. What two images seem to predominate in poetry of solitude? Do these images tend to be absolute in their meaning, or does their meaning have a different value with different writers?
3. Does folk-rock have its own set of unwritten rules about form and contents? Does poetry? Use the section on Crosby (and any other) as a basis for your discussion.

Section 11: Stephen Stills
For What It's Worth

1. a) What contribution does the *form* of each selection in this unit make to its meaning?
   b) Are there certain forms of poetry that lend themselves more readily to the expression of pessimism and fear? (*e.g.* Is free verse better for this than structured verse? Is acid-rock, folk-rock or rock 'n roll better for this than traditional forms?)

Section 12: Paul Simon
Old Friends

1. a) "Poetry on the subject of old age seems to share a common atmosphere, and a similarity in diction and imagery." Investigate the selections in this section to see if this statement has some truth.
   b) Look in other poetry anthologies for poems dealing with old age in different ways. (*e.g.* Yeats: *An Acre of Grass;* Tennyson: *Ulysses;* Souster: *The Top Hat.*) Is the atmosphere, the type of imagery, and the diction much different from that of the poems in this book?
2. What dimension is added to the picture of old age by presenting it in *song*? (In your opinion, could any other singers in this book have done *Old Friends* in the same way that Simon and Garfunkel do it?)

Section 13: Mick Jagger
Paint It Black

1. Of all the selections in this unit, *Paint It Black* is clearly the most powerful, even without the supporting music. Why is this so?
Lady Jane
2. Read again the part of the introduction that deals with *Lady Jane.* Do you agree that the speaker is a cad?
3. In your opinion is *The Indifferent* sincere or insincere?

Section 15: Harry Nilsson
1941

1. The introduction suggests that another dimension is added to Nilsson's *1941* by what he does *not* say. Does this statement apply as well to the poem by Cummings?

Without Her
2. Do Shelley's and Byron's poems appear contrived when juxtaposed with Nilsson's *Without Her*?
3. Nilsson has been accused of stringing together a series of clichés in *Without Her*. Do you agree?

Section 16: Bob Lind
Elusive Butterfly of Love
1. What features of technique do poems and lyrics share when they deal with something vague?

Section 17: Leonard Cohen
1. Leonard Cohen is admired as a poet whose work has appeal for *everyone*. What in his writing appeals to you? Is there anything in his style of writing or in his philosophy that does not appeal to you?
2. The National Film Board of Canada has made an outstanding documentary film on Cohen called *Ladies and Gentlemen: Mr. Leonard Cohen*. If you have the good fortune to be able to view this film, try to estimate to what degree it is in harmony with Cohen's poetry.
Suzanne
3. Who is Suzanne?
4. How close does *Peter Quince at the Clavier* come to summing up the feeling that people experience when they listen to Cohen singing *Suzanne*?
5. What tenets of Taoism do you see in *Suzanne*?
Teachers
6. Each of the selections in this unit deals with man's place in the cosmos—his reason for existence, and his relationship with all other forms of existence.
a) Do any of the poems by Laotse or Pope present a satisfactory reaction to the problems posed in *Teachers*?
b) Point out the similarities in theme between *Teachers* and *The Bear on the Delhi Road*.
c) How do you feel Cohen would react to Spender's *What I Expected* or FitzGerald's *Rubaiyat*?
d) Which poem in this unit is most similar to *Teachers* in narrative method?
Stranger Song
7. Each of the selections in this unit uses a different type of imagery to convey the ephemeral quality of human relationships. Describe the imagery used in each selection. Which poems, in your opinion, are most successful?

Discography

You Don't Know My Mind
Josh White
Josh White
Elektra 123

Fixing to Die
Bukka White
Bukka White Vol. 1
Tokoma 1001
Country Blues 1
Folkways RF 1
Buffy Sainte-Marie
Many a Mile
Vanguard 79171

**Mose
My Neighborhood
Don't Pat Me on the Back
and Call Me Brother
Just Look In My Face**
John KaSandra
John KaSandra
Capitol ST 2957

Tom Joad
Woody Guthrie
Dust Bowl Ballads
Folkways FH 5212

Hard Travellin'
Woody Guthrie
Woody Guthrie
Folkways FA 2483

**The Ballad of the Carpenter
The First Time Ever
I Saw Your Face**
Ewan MacColl
New Britain Gazette (1)
Folkways FW 8732

Crucifixion
Phil Ochs
Pleasures of the Harbor
A & M 4133

His Name Is Andrew
Dave Ackles
Dave Ackles
Elektra 74022

The Dove
Judy Collins
In My Life
Elektra 74027

**Little Boxes
What Have They Done to the Rain?
God Bless the Grass**
Malvina Reynolds
*Malvina Reynolds Sings
the Truth*
Columbia CS 9414

The Half-Masted Schooner
Bruce MacKay
Bruce MacKay
Oro-1069

**The Sacraments of Evil
Song of the Black Veils**
Bruce MacKay
Bruce MacKay Is
Gamma GS 501

Mind Gardens
The Byrds
Younger than Yesterday
Columbia CS 9442

For What It's Worth
The Buffalo Springfield
Buffalo Springfield
Atco SD 33-200

Old Friends
Simon and Garfunkel
Bookends
Columbia KCS 9529

**Paint It Black
Lady Jane**
The Rolling Stones
Aftermath
London 476

Ruby Tuesday
The Rolling Stones
Between the Buttons
London 499

Strange Brew
The Cream
Disraeli Gears
Atco (S) 33-232

1941
Without Her
Harry Nilsson
Pandemonium Shadow Show
RCA Victor LSP 3874

Elusive Butterfly of Love
Bob Lind
Don't Be Concerned
World Pacific 77808

Suzanne
Teachers
The Stranger Song
Sisters of Mercy
Leonard Cohen
Songs of Leonard Cohen
Columbia CS 9533

I'm Going Home on
the Morning Train
The Cities are Burning
The Rev. Frederick Kirkpatrick
Everybody's Got a
Right to Live
Broadside BR 308
Pete Seeger
Pete Seeger Now
Columbia CS 9717

I Have a Dream
The Rev. Dr. Martin Luther King
The March on Washington—
The Official Album
Radio Station WRVJ,
New York, New York

Acknowledgments

An Elementary School Class Room in a Slum by Stephen Spender reprinted from *Collected Poems* by permission of Faber and Faber Ltd. and Alfred A. Knopf Inc.

Frederick Douglass by Robert Hayden reprinted from *Selected Poems* by permission of October House. Copyright 1966 by Robert Hayden.

I Think Continually by Stephen Spender from *Collected Poems* by permission of Faber and Faber Ltd. and Alfred A. Knopf Inc.

nobody loses all the time by E. E. Cummings reprinted from *Poems, 1923-1954* by permission of Harcourt, Brace & World Inc. Copyright 1926 by Horace Liveright; renewed 1954 by E. E. Cummings.

The Southern Road by Dudley Randall reprinted from *New Negro Poets: USA*, edited by Langston Hughes, by permission of Indiana University Press.

The Send-Off by Wilfred Owen reprinted from *Collected Poems of Wilfred Owen* by permission of Mr. Harold Owen, Chatto and Windus Ltd., and New Directions Publishing Inc.

Arms and the Boy by Wilfred Owen reprinted from *Collected Poems of Wilfred Owen* by Permission of Mr. Harold Owen, Chatto and Windus Ltd., and New Directions Publishing Inc.

The Unknown Citizen by W. H. Auden reprinted from *Collected Shorter Poems, 1927-1957* by permission of Faber and Faber Ltd. and Random House Inc. Copyright 1940 and renewed 1968 by W. H. Auden.

Warren Pryor by Alden Nowlan reprinted from *Under the Ice* by permission of The Ryerson Press, Toronto.

The End of the World by Archibald MacLeish reprinted from *Collected Poems, 1917-1952* by permission of Archibald MacLeish and Houghton Mifflin Company.

Letter to the President by Walter Lowenfels reprinted by permission of the author.

Mater Dolorosa by Karen Lindsey reprinted from *Kauri* and *Where Is Vietnam? American Poets Respond*, by permission of the author.

Prologue by Yevgeny Yevtushenko reprinted from *The Poetry of Yevgeny Yevtushenko*, revised and enlarged edition, edited, translated, with an introduction by George Reavey, by permission of October House Inc. Copyright 1965, 1967 by George Reavey.

The Landscape Near an Aerodrome by Stephen Spender reprinted from *Collected Poems, 1928-1953* by permission of Alfred A. Knopf Inc.

The Snow Man by Wallace Stevens reprinted from *Collected Poems of Wallace Stevens* by permission of Alfred A. Knopf Inc. Copyright 1923 and renewed 1951 by Wallace Stevens.

Living for Others by Laotse from *The Wisdom of Laotse*, edited by Lin Yutang, reprinted by permission of Alfred A. Knopf Inc. Copyright 1948 by Random House Inc.

For the Fallen by Laurence Binyon reprinted by permission of The Society of Authors for the Estate of Laurence Binyon.

To the Glorious Dead by Judi Vyse reprinted by permission of the author.

What Were They Like? by Denise Levertov reprinted from *The Nation*, 27 June 1966, by permission of the author and *The Nation*.

The Road by James Stephens reprinted from *Songs of the Clay* by permission of Mrs. Iris Wise and Macmillan & Co. Ltd., London; and The Macmillan Company of Canada Ltd.

Truth by Uta Peikert reprinted by permission of the author.

A Ritual to Read to Each Other by William Stafford reprinted by permission of the author.

A Kingdom for Mr. Bojangles by Penelope Schafer reprinted by permission of the author.

Mr. Flood's Party by Edwin Arlington Robinson reprinted from *Collected Poems* by permission of The Macmillan Company of Canada Ltd. Copyright 1921 by Edwin Arlington Robinson and renewed 1949 by Ruth Nivison.

When I See Old Men by Raymond Souster reprinted from *The Colour of the Times* by permission of The Ryerson Press, Toronto.

Promise of Peace by Robinson Jeffers reprinted by permission of Messrs. Donnan and Garth Jeffers.

On the Move by Thom Gunn from *The Sense of Movement* reprinted by permission of Faber and Faber Ltd.

anyone lived in a pretty how town by E. E. Cummings reprinted from *Poems, 1923-1954* by permission of Harcourt, Brace & World Inc. Copyright 1940 by E. E. Cummings; renewed 1968 by Marion Morehouse Cummings.

Manifestations of Tao by Laotse from *The Wisdom of Laotse*, edited by Lin Yutang, reprinted by permission of Alfred A. Knopf Inc. Copyright 1948 by Random House Inc.

Peter Quince at the Clavier by Wallace Stevens reprinted by permission of Faber and Faber Ltd. and Alfred A. Knopf Inc.

Water by Laotse from *The Wisdom of Laotse*, edited by Lin Yutang, reprinted by permission of Alfred A. Knopf Inc. Copyright 1948 by Random House Inc.

The Spirit of the Valley by Laotse from *The Wisdom of Laotse*, edited by Lin Yutang, reprinted by permission of Alfred A. Knopf Inc. Copyright 1948 by Random House Inc.

Futility of Contention by Laotse reprinted from *The Wisdom of Laotse*, edited by Lin Yutang, by permission of Alfred A. Knopf Inc. Copyright 1948 by Random House Inc.

The Bear on the Delhi Road by Earle Birney reprinted by permission of McClelland & Stewart, Toronto.

What I Expected by Stephen Spender reprinted from *Collected Poems, 1928-1953* by permission of Faber and Faber Ltd.

Conquering the World of Inaction by Laotse reprinted from *The Wisdom of Laotse,* edited by Lin Yutang, reprinted by permission of Alfred A. Knopf Inc. Copyright 1948 by Random House Inc.

The Nameless Ones by Conrad Aiken reprinted from *Collected Poems* by permission of Oxford University Press Inc. Copyright 1953 by Conrad Aiken.

The Force That Through the Green Fuse . . . by Dylan Thomas reprinted from *The Collected Poems of Dylan Thomas* by permission of New Directions Publishing Corp. Copyright 1939 by New Directions Publishing Corp.

En Una Noche Oscura by Saint John of the Cross, translated by Roy Cambell, reprinted by permission of the Roy Cambell Estate and Harvill Press Ltd.

A Dead Man Asks for a Drink by St. Denys Garneau, translated by F. R. Scott, reprinted by permission of F. R. Scott.

Embracing the One by Laotse from *The Wisdom of Laotse,* edited by Lin Yutang, reprinted by permission of Alfred A. Knopf Inc. Copyright 1948 by Random House Inc.

Every step has been taken to make this list of acknowledgements complete; but in some cases all efforts to reach the copyright holder failed. All errors and omissions drawn to our attention will be corrected in future editions.

Photograph credits: Frontispiece, Miller Services Ltd.; facing page 1, Szilasi Gabor; page 12, Bill Smith — Coda Magazine; page 18, Capitol Records; page 36, Dorothea Lange for the Farm Security Administration; page 52, Dan Seeger; page 60 A&M Records; page 66, Elektra Records; page 72, Miller Services Ltd.; page 74, U.S. Army Photographer; page 82, Colombia Records; page 98, Paskal; page 104, U.S. Information Agency; pages 114 and 120, Atlantic Records; page 136 and 150, Miller Services Ltd.; page 156, Nilsson Productions; page 160, BART; page 164, National Film Board — M. Semale; page 168, Columbia Records; page 192, Jim Loomis; page 194, United Press International.

Index of Themes

Index